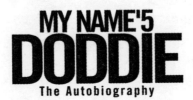

MY NAME'5
DODDIE

The Autobiography

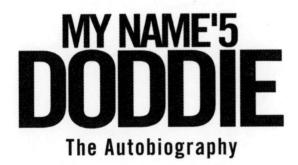

MY NAME'5 DODDIE

The Autobiography

DODDIE WEIR

with Stewart Weir

BLACK & WHITE PUBLISHING

First published in 2018
by Black & White Publishing Ltd
Nautical House, 104 Commercial Street
Edinburgh EH6 6NF

3 5 7 9 10 8 6 4 2   18 19 20 21

Reprinted 2018

ISBN: 978 1 78530 224 4

Typeset by Iolaire, Newtonmore
Printed and bound by CPI Group (UK) Ltd, Croydon, CR0 4YY

To Kathy, Hamish, Angus and Ben, and to everyone else who has helped me have such a good time.

Contents

Foreword

JIM TELFER

'D GIVEN UP COACHING after the '84 Grand Slam because I had a new job in teaching, and then in 1988 I'd returned to coach Scotland's forwards. The following year, Melrose weren't doing so well in the league and I went back to give the coach a helping hand and see if we could avoid relegation, which we did.

That's when I first met Doddie Weir. He was eighteen and I'd never really seen anyone, or anything, like him.

He was quite skinny and tall, a huge gangling laddie who became a bigger man and player.

So, Melrose avoided the drop, and from there went on to achieve great things. That team had a bunch of players who were quite outstanding. They didn't all get to play for their country, but the ones who did were exceptional, and Doddie was among them.

When I arrived back at Melrose, my nephew, Carl Hogg, had suffered some quite bad shoulder injuries, and there was a worry that some young players were not physically strong enough to be subjected to too many scrums at senior level. Doddie's dad, Jock, was a wee bit apprehensive about him playing in the second row, but I just wanted him, so we played him at number 8, although he was always destined to be a lock forward.

He played at 8, and he had great mobility, but I never thought his handling from the scrum was great. Doddie's height meant that he had to go a long way down to pick the ball up. I always felt that was a hindrance, but as a line-out jumper, he was immense. He was tall, but he could out-jump players of a comparable height, and bigger. Doddie had a natural spring about him.

For me, having coached Melrose and Scotland for years, without having any real ability in line-out play, Doddie was a godsend. When he came into the reckoning for Scotland, what a bonus it was. At last, we had someone who jumped up, not down!

Doddie would win your own ball – he had terrific hands to catch, tip and deflect – but he would contest the opposition throw and, jumping at the front of the line-out, he was a real obstacle and put real pressure on the opposition hooker if he was trying to drop the ball in the middle or at the tail of the line.

When there were the various rule changes, regarding lifting and assisting, you could still literally throw Doddie into the air and keep him there because he wasn't carrying too much weight. And he was very mobile – hence the infamous comment about him running like a young giraffe on the charge, all arms and legs, and looking almost uncoordinated at times. But that perception of him as all over the place was wholly unfair.

People might have been taken in by that description, and by Doddie's antics. However, the reality was we had a supremely talented rugby player and athlete. Just think how good a Sevens player he was.

Doddie has always had a switch he can flick on and off. Off, and he's the village idiot, loud – very loud – gregarious, doing daft things like nudging you when you're off balance, or grabbing you and sticking his finger in your ear – although he was never as annoying, or caused as much mayhem as, say, Gary Armstrong or Bryan Redpath. I blame it on him growing up in the middle of nowhere, talking to sheep. I've told him that. When he meets folk, he goes bananas. He's just so pleased to see them.

But when that switch was on, as a rugby player, whether with club or country, Doddie was a completely different animal: focused, concentrated, confident, a huge presence, ferociously proud and committed, and immensely physical. He might have appeared skinny, but those long legs and arms gave him tremendous leverage. That's what gave him his strength, not working on the farm. I don't think he did that much actual farm work, regardless of what he says.

I've often thought that Doddie became a rugby player because that's what was presented to him, either through his family or school, and because of the environment he grew up in. But had he been introduced to athletics at an early age, you could see him as a four-hundred-metres runner, with that huge loping stride, or as a swimmer: again, using those big levers to pull him fast through the water. Be in no doubt about Doddie being an athlete.

It was no surprise that, when the professional era dawned,

Doddie was quickly recruited. If it hadn't been Newcastle, it would have been someone else. He took to the 'open' game like a natural. And within a couple of years he was headed for South Africa with the Lions.

Remember, that was the first tour of the professional era, and Doddie made it on that trip, against excellent competition in that position, to face the world champions.

And he didn't look out of place alongside seasoned 'pros' such as ex-League boys like Tait, Gibbs, Bentley, Bateman, Young and Quinnell. It would have been a great tour, had it not been for the clinical brutality shown towards Doddie against Mpumalanga at Witbank.

That brutality denied Doddie the chance to compete for a Test place, but we were left with one of the classic Lions moments, when during a media training exercise before we left for South Africa, he was 'accused' of breaking a curfew, having been spotted in a bar.

Famously, Doddie claimed it was 'mistaken identity' and that his father was on tour as well. Everyone laughed at his one-liner – comedy genius! I thought it was hilarious for a different reason: if you know Doddie and his father Jock, they are very different shapes – really no chance there of mistaken identity.

Last year, Doddie went on another Lions tour, to New Zealand. It was as he made his way there with his family that I found out from my sister, Sheila, about Doddie's condition. I was shocked; I think we all are still.

It's a challenge for all concerned, especially Doddie. But, like helping Melrose avoid relegation, breaking into the Scotland squad as a teenager, embracing professionalism and moving to England, and overcoming the disappointment of South Africa and a potentially career-threatening injury, Doddie is meeting MND like every other test he's confronted. Head on.

And we are all right behind him.

MY NAME'5
DODDIE
The Autobiography

1

Not the Christmas
I Was Expecting

DECEMBER 23RD, 2016. A Friday. Only the Saturday left for any last-minute Christmas shopping. Being honest, I wasn't even thinking that far ahead, and, as we made our way up to Edinburgh, I don't suppose Kathy was either.

A year before, in November 2015, I'd started having problems with my left hand. Some time earlier, and I can't be sure exactly when because it was so inconsequential, I'd jammed it in a gate and injured it, but I'd done that kind of thing before, working around the farm and the likes, so didn't really give it much of a second thought. But after a little while, I became aware that I didn't have the power in it I should have, but I thought it would come back, once it fixed itself. Why wouldn't it?

I'd had this kind of injury before and nothing came of it. It would heal through time. But I didn't appear to have the same grip I'd always had. Then my skin began twitching, involuntary twitches. I'd never felt or experienced anything like that. Computer on, symptoms typed in.

Oh . . .

Quite literally, it was an 'oh f***' moment. I'm not one who swears a great deal, but I can almost remember hissing it. Of course, I didn't realise at the time what it all meant, or have the understanding and knowledge I have now. Otherwise it would have been an even bigger 'oh f***' moment, and I quite possibly might have screamed it too.

But what would I do next? Going online and looking up various ailments or illnesses. We've all done it. Actually, until that moment, I'd never done it. Maybe I'd got it wrong. What if I had?

'I think I might have Motor Neurone Disease.'

It isn't really something you can drop easily into a conversation. Not even if your next line is:

'But don't panic as I might be wrong.'

Although that was something along the lines of the conversation I had with Kathy.

'Let's get Christmas and New Year out the way first (as you do), and then we'll think about it,' she said.

Except, every time I went to use my hand, I couldn't do anything but think about it.

Eventually I went to see my own doctor, who didn't hang around and referred me immediately to see the specialist.

And so the tests began. This was in the following June – blood tests, shock therapy, more blood taken, and lumbar punctures. That last one was a shocker. A nurse came in and asked if she could do my lumbar puncture.

'Fine,' I said. 'How many have you done?'

'Only the one.'

Now, that one might have been the greatest ever example

of a lumbar puncture being performed, but this was a big deal for me. It wasn't that I was thinking I wanted it done properly. It was just that I didn't want to feel that nervous or anxious while it was being performed. At which point I asked if someone else might be available.

One of her colleagues then came in to perform the procedure, but even with him, it was an absolutely hellish experience. I ended up with ten times the anaesthetic I should have had, simply because the needle wouldn't go through the tissue in my back, which despite me not playing for a dozen years, was still solid. Who'd have thought?

But, it wasn't something I'd recommend.

I wasn't a great fan of the MRI scan either. It put me in mind of getting stuck in a barrel once while we were doing some team bonding. Being blindfolded at the same time was supposed to relax you, but it only heightened the apprehension.

Apparently, I was diagnosed quite quickly, but don't be misled by the use of the word quickly. There is no single test for MND. It's not like a blood test, or a smear, or a sample that gives you the key indicators. No, this 'quick' diagnosis means you go through the whole gamut of everything a forty-something could have, covering the entire spectrum of illnesses and conditions, just to rule them all out, one by one, until you arrive at an outcome and a result you don't particularly want to know.

Being honest, I think I knew what I had – ever since I googled it. For once, trying to be clever meant that instead of finding out from a doctor or a consultant what was wrong, I was only looking for confirmation from the experts. All the tests and examinations were necessary, however, but they were still only a build-up to what I had already suspected for a year – the inevitable news that I had MND.

And that was the message that was delivered that Friday afternoon right before Christmas 2016.

Me being me, I was always pessimistic during my rugby career. *I won't be selected, I won't be in the team, I'll be dropped.* Then, *Oh you beauty, I've been picked, get in there!* Convincing myself something bad would happen always prepared me for the worst. Then if the worst turned out to be good news – result!

Unfortunately, the result that day in Edinburgh was what I expected, but not what I wanted. It was MND. Motor Neurone Disease. Kathy – my wife, 'Mary Doll' as I always call her – was shocked, devastated. You can put a brave face on, but in that initial moment, you are not kidding anyone. If you are not emotional, it's probably through fear or utter shock, or both.

There is no nice way of telling someone they have MND. But in my experience, there are some not-so-nice ways of delivering bad news. The way the prognosis was delivered, I found cold. I asked what the timescale was. I thought, maybe he's just as upset; maybe my question will break the ice. Maybe he will reel off a list of dos and don'ts; maybe he'll tell me to try walking, try swimming, try drinking, eating; maybe he'll tell me don't drink, don't eat certain things.

Instead he replied, with some confidence, that I wouldn't be walking in here in a year from now. Chilling that, in terms of the consequences and his delivery.

If he said that to give me a goal, who knows, he might be some kind of psychology genius. I don't know, but it didn't sound like it.

More than eighteen months on, we're well past that deadline. And I'm still walking, still talking – talking more than ever – and living life to the full, although holding pint glasses and doing up ties and buttons is proving very difficult. I've learned to compromise. Beer, wine, champagne, whisky: they all taste the same, regardless of the glass, regardless of if it's the wrong glass.

But I was still walking last Christmas, and that consultant said I wouldn't be. I win that one. Whether it is a Pyrrhic victory, time will tell.

To go back to that Friday in Edinburgh, just when you think you can't be more shocked – and, remember, Kathy was in bits at this point – suddenly you are introduced to someone who will be your care nurse and told that it's time to 'say hello' to them. And you do, because it isn't their fault either that you have this disease or that they've been invited in to share the news.

And that was it. Actually, it wasn't. I was also told there was a lot of information to be had on the internet. Was that the same internet I'd consulted to find out what could be causing that twitching?

This advice comes when your brain is in meltdown, trying to get some kind of handle on the consequences, when you're running through scenarios like the fastest computer in the world.

Kathy, kids, farm, mortgage, three kids, car lease, business, *just how long do I have*, Hamish, Angus, Ben, Kathy, what will she do, my mum, dad, my family, employees, lambing, my rugby friends, the boys.

Then I think maybe the consultant has been saying things while I have been away on a different planet, attempting to make sense of what I'm being told. He hasn't. He doesn't really have much to say.

I look at Kathy. All she does is stare. I think we were frightened to look at each other at the same time. Still, we know who the care nurse is and, thank goodness, we have the internet. All of which, to my mind, just wasn't enough.

Thankfully, I could go and speak to a friend in Newcastle, Graham Wylie, who has always been very supportive of where we are, and who knew a chap by the name of Tim Williams, a consultant neurologist in Newcastle.

It was Tim who gave me an A4 piece of paper, all very informative, very helpful.

It said this is the drug you should be taking, Riluzole, and you should be taking it with x, y and z, you should be eating a, b and c, and try this, this and that. It doesn't sound much. But it was. It was a bit of positivity, a bit of light in what was a very dark tunnel.

Even so, it wasn't a very bright light, and it still isn't.

Riluzole is the only drug available in this country for the treatment of MND. One drug. And that was introduced more than twenty-odd years ago. Compare that to the treatments, medicines, pills and potions available for other illnesses. Surely there should be something else out there, and if there isn't, is there a way of finding something, or someone, interested in this field?

My desperation, my need for answers, was the planting

of the seed, so to speak, of what I would try and do, for me and for fellow MND sufferers.

Sitting, waiting for the inevitable, just wasn't an option. We needed to get things up and running, get some movement in terms of positivity and direction. That would take time I might not have.

But, when you are desperate, it's amazing how quickly you can move.

2

In the Beginning

I MIGHT AS WELL SET something straight from the outset. I wasn't always this size. Just like some of you, I was a child once upon a time. There's even the photographic evidence to prove it.

I was born on the 4th of July, 1970, and all the United States of America celebrated, which was nice. All my life, people have given a nod of approval, or a wee smile, whenever I give my date of birth. I'd have missed out on those little gestures had I been a day early, or a day late. It's one of those unforgettable birthdays, which has helped people remember that they need to get me a card, or a present, or both.

So, that's me: George Wilson Weir, first born out of Jock and Nanny Weir (without wanting to make them sound too much like racehorses), although there hangs a tale, even in the name. I'm named after my grandfather, not that Mum was terribly pleased at that. But under the circumstances, she couldn't really say too much about it. And that's why the 'Doddie' moniker stuck quite early in my childhood; now it's been around for a long time.

I never knew my grandfather Weir. He was a butcher in Stow, before moving to Cortleferry Farm, but he died when my dad was just eleven. From that point on, Dad took over the running of the farm. According to him, he'd have played more for Gala had he not been so committed to the farm. That's his story, although other theories are available. But seriously, Old Jock does produce the odd programme from yesteryear every now and again, just to prove that he was once a player. I'm not sure his evidence would hold up in court, but I have seen his name in old newspaper clippings, playing for Gala alongside the likes of Drew Gill, Arthur Brown, Dunky Paterson and packing down with a certain PC Brown at number 8.

At Gala, Jock Weir's contemporaries would have been the likes of Ken Macaulay and Tom Smith. Dad was a big unit himself, six foot four inches, and a bit of weight behind him as well. But then again, Saturdays were working days for those in agriculture. If you got someone to cover you, it either cost money or you had to repay the favour yourself. As a result, Dad played more for Gala YM.

In rugby terms, I think what really rubbed off on me from Dad were the friendships he developed through the game. Playing was great, as was going on the odd trip. But the people he met lasted longer than his career and, for me, that has been just as important during my career as it was to him. He still meets up with his fellow old boys now, which unfortunately usually means a bad head the next day. It must be hereditary.

But back to the expanding Weir brood. A year after my big entrance, on the 20th of July 1971, I became a big brother to a little sister with the arrival of Kirsty – not that wee now, but there you are – and then in 1974, Thomas made his big entrance, on the 11th of July.

Other people might look into family trees and their ancestry. Me, I've always been meaning to do a bit of research into what the hell was happening at the Young Farmers dances back then, or what they were serving at the bar! Three kids, all born in July, is some strike rate.

For a few years it all went quiet – I almost said horribly wrong – until my youngest brother, Christopher, arrived on the scene, but not until 1984, and not in July. The old farmers dances obviously weren't as good by the 1980s. We were, and still are, as close as most siblings, although Christopher – because of the age gap – wasn't party to some of the things we got up to as youngsters and teenagers, but thankfully he caught us up, probably around the time he could buy alcohol, legally.

Christopher was farmed out as a baby, and even as a bigger baby, to very good friends, Bill and Agnes Mathison, neighbouring farm workers and still with us. Mum and Agnes would meet every Monday – they still do – and are really good friends, a friendship that goes back forty years. So, because Kirsty and I were heavily involved in the horses, Christopher was left behind (in a few ways) and spent many of his weekends with the Mathisons, which meant Bill and Agnes semi-adopted him.

To this day, Bill still comes around the farm. He's retired – and has been for twenty years – except, like so many who've worked on the land, you never quite retire. We'd be totally lost without him – Bill must have put up about

50,000 metres of fencing around the farm. You didn't think that was me, did you? It's been done properly.

They did it properly in those early days when they were looking after Christopher, too. With them not having kids, Bill and Agnes would be checking on him every hour when he was asleep, and if he didn't move for a minute or two, they'd give him a poke just to make sure he was okay!

Christopher was christened Christopher Paterson, which is Agnes's maiden name, a nice thank you for all their hard work. And, let's face it, he must have been hard work.

When Bill and Agnes went to Blackpool, they took Christopher. When Mum was away, Christopher would stay with his 'reserve' parents. That relationship has only got stronger through time, especially in later years, with Christopher using his 'home from home' as a way of procuring food.

Mum's mince and tatties and stew were great. But let's just say her repertoire was somewhat limited (unless it came from Marks & Spencer). We found that out even more once we'd spread our wings and been introduced to the world's menu of pizza, pasta, curries and the likes.

If Christopher wasn't happy as a kid with the fare on offer at home, he'd jump on his wee 50cc Honda motorbike and head off over the fields to Agnes who would spoil him rotten. A few times the rest of us also thought that wasn't a bad idea and there would be a scramble to see who could get to the cottage first. Agnes was a great baker and cook, so there was always something to look forward to. Sorry, Mum.

Mum was a Houston from Cupar, and her family was

involved in engineering and fabrication, having started out as blacksmiths. I may well have picked up some of my sporting genes from my grandfather on Mum's side. Bert was a goalkeeper in his day, but also a very good cricketer with Cupar Cricket Club.

Once Mum's schooling was out of the way, she became a nanny – hence why she's called Nanny to this day, even though her name is Margaret. While her culinary skills left something to be desired (although she did prepare the stuff out of Marks & Sparks beautifully), as you would expect from someone who made a living and a career in the early days out of looking after other folks' weans, she was a wonderful mother to her growing brood.

It was a good thing at the time. But, looking back, I'd go so far as to say that Mum has never stopped mothering us. That was partly my own fault because I left her to it. But until I left home to sign for Newcastle, I don't think I'd ever booked my own dentist's or doctor's appointment, or packed my own bag, or done my own washing. I wasn't lazy, but while I was still thinking about it, she had it already done. She wasn't one for letting folk get in her way when things needed doing. When I went on tours, I had the most immaculately packed bags – and often Agnes would help out too. But after day one on tour, my bags weren't quite as neat and tidy.

Mum was protective and still is; Dad was encouraging, and still is. Chalk and cheese in their approach to life in many ways, but no less supportive or loving.

When I was younger, I wasn't into rugby. Equestrianism was my first love, something passed down from my mum.

Now, that takes serious money, in terms of getting horses, keeping them, feeding them, stabling them, veterinary bills, even the transportation, diesel, entry fees and the likes. Dad would always be supportive when it came to paying the bills and taking an interest in what Kirsty and I were about, and he was there when he was needed.

But, like Dad's rugby, having the time to be there was never that easy. For my part, with the boys, I've always tried to be there for them in whatever they might be doing. Circumstances mean I'm really conscientious about making that effort now. But it is never easy when you have work and business commitments, especially during the school term.

Maybe my experiences have taught me to look more towards my family. Different mindset today, I know, plus I was a professional rugby player and then into a nine-to-five job after that, compared to my father, who was twelve hours a day, solid, and eighteen hours at some times in the year.

Very seldom did we have family holidays. I think that's something that is a bit of a trait within the farming community. There isn't an off-season on the farm; something is always happening and that means you, especially if you own or run the farm, have to be there all year round. And in my case as a kid, that meant Dad. As a result, we rarely went anywhere en masse.

I think the first holiday my parents had, after their honeymoon, may have been to Spittal or somewhere like that. I don't think they had been on a plane until they flew out to South Africa in 1997 to see me – and of course I wasn't there by the time they arrived, as we'll see later.

If they did go anywhere, then it was certainly done for us, the children, to give us an experience or something new and different. And that couldn't have been easy with the commitment they had to the farm.

But we did get away. Occasionally to Blackpool – see, it's not just the folk from the big smokes who enjoy the Las Vegas of the North – and those were great adventures and expeditions, to the St Ives Hotel.

As a child, or up to a certain age at least, I don't think you get what a holiday means. It seems a lot of upheaval and for what – to be taken away from all the things in your life, friends, toys, bikes? Once you've been on one or two, then you get the hang of it and discover that it is quite exciting and something different and, therefore, to be enjoyed. And we did enjoy the arcades and rides and the beach and the sea and the prom. All a bit different from our usual haunts and surrounds in the Borders.

What was also different, as we headed for the surf and sand, was our attire. For some reason, Mother thought Thomas and me would look best in a shirt, tie and shorts. On the beach in Blackpool. Needless to say, we had that look all to ourselves.

Summer, for me, is for holidays – stress-free, feet-up time, and a time to see how your children are developing into big people. Giving them some of the experiences rugby was good enough to give me. Going on flights, seeing sights, eating different food, trying to communicate.

Actually, if you take the flights bit out of that, it's a bit like going to Selkirk.

But, in hindsight, we were actually having holidays every

weekend just about, because we were away with the horses, going to competitions here, shows there, a brilliant lifestyle. Again, while we might have been deprived of summer holidays compared to some, they probably didn't own a horse, or get to ride one. The closest they'd get to equestrianism would be back to Blackpool and a go on the donkeys.

We went to a little primary school, Fountainhall Primary, about a mile and a half from the farm. I think it must have been quite unique in that it had a massive twenty-six kids between primary 1 and primary 7. Looking back, they were good times, with the Hendry family, who we see from time to time, the Thomsons, Colin and Andrew, who we don't really see now.

I'm not sure – not that I spend time worrying about it or analysing it in detail – if that had any effect on me as a kid, because I was quite shy. I can hear you laughing again, but I was. Or was it because I wasn't very clever?

So it came as a bit of a culture shock when I was packed off to Stewart's Melville in Edinburgh, when I was in primary 6. We were remote, on the farm, in the middle of nowhere, and, as I said, I was at school with a couple of dozen kids, who I knew everything about. There aren't many secrets when you are that close-knit. But aged nine or ten, other than my family and school mates, I didn't see anyone else very much. The nearest shop, the post office in Stow, would be five miles away, Galashiels twelve miles. Only occasionally would you go there.

To then be confronted by five or six hundred kids at Stewart's Melville, I really had never experienced anything like that before. It was a jolt to the system. Did I have difficulty in adjusting? Again, without getting too hung up on it, it wasn't something I was instantly comfortable with. Even now, I'm happiest on my farm with the family, out the road, away from the hustle and bustle of town life. I think that's a throwback to how I was raised.

There was so much of school life that I just found utterly alien and quite weird, what with the uniform, which included the blazer – and short trousers when you attended the primary school. I didn't like that. And then when I got used to the shorts and was happy wearing them, I had to wear long trousers at senior school, which I didn't really like either. I know these seem like minuscule issues, but they caused me a bit of grief.

I was a day pupil at Stew Mel. Maybe that should be a long-day pupil. We started early, crack of dawn stuff, because rather than the bus there, we would get a lift up to Edinburgh with Graham Brown, who played rugby for Kelso (where he was nicknamed 'Smiler'), and played a bit of tennis as well. He was one of the teachers at Stew Mel, and he gave me and Kirsty – who also eventually went there – a lift to school each morning. He came from Stow, but when he'd pick us up in the winter, we'd be frozen getting in the car, and never really thawed out because the heater in his old Ford Fiesta wasn't great.

Graham Brown got us there, but we came back on the bus, the number 95 to Hawick. And there were a few coming back down the road to keep us company. Quite a few of the kids from the farms went to Stew Mel, I don't know why, but we would come home with other children off different farms, like the Rosses of Wester Middleton. Michael, Mark and Jackie were a similar age to ourselves – there has to have been something going on at these Young Farmers dos around that time. Douglas Helm, at Haltree Farm (but who attended Edinburgh Academy), is another around the same age as us. I really will have to make enquiries.

Anyway, school days were long days. School, especially secondary school for me, was an occupational hazard. You had to do it, but I was more interested in filling the tractor up with diesel, or getting my horse ready for a meeting, than I ever was in learning. I must have picked up some things, to get through agricultural college. But it was never something I grew to like.

One thing Stewart's Melville did do was give me an interest in rugby. But it was no more than a passing interest. I played, and was quite good, but was I ever driven to become a great player? No, not really. But the fact that I ever progressed in rugby owes so much – almost everything, in fact – to my beloved sister.

I was always involved with horses, riding around the farm, where I'd practise jumping and staying on. Riding about just rounding up sheep wouldn't interest me. I needed a competitive edge, a challenge, someone to compete against.

We were competing in gymkhanas and pony club competitions – all the usual tests of riding, throwing, catching and the likes. I do think that helped my hand-eye coordination for playing rugby. Be honest, trying to catch a rugby ball while being jostled at a line-out is probably easier than catching a tennis ball while being bounced around on a pony.

Eventually I'd outgrow the ponies. It was a bit

embarrassing when other kids were having to jump off their horse to retrieve a ball or a baton, but I could just lean down and pick it up. More embarrassing was kicking the fences down when it was my long legs, not the horse, knocking the poles off. Time to move up to something bigger, both in terms of the horse and the level of competition.

But Kirsty and I – Tom was never interested – really enjoyed ourselves riding horses, especially at the likes of the Thirlestane Horse Trial, and she has passed that love of the sport on to her own daughter.

One day, years later, my nieces, Alex Mundell and Charlotte Dun, found these show-jumping trophies that had their uncle Dodgy's name on them. I think they thought I'd been kidding when I said I was good!

The best part of my equestrian career came in tandem with a wonderful horse, Arpal Glider. He was just such an intelligent beast, and we really connected. He would do things almost on instinct, but always the right thing. Very clever, and he pulled me out of a few disasters along the way.

However, my eventing and show-jumping career came to an abrupt and sad end.

I would do many of the Common Riding events around the Borders (I'll explain more later), but one day Kirsty asked if she could take Arpal Glider and do the Gala ride. It was that time of year and I was helping Dad with the sheep and the clipping, so off Kirsty went, only to return, horseless.

Going up a hill, the horse died underneath her. Thankfully she wasn't hurt, but I was. I had lost a great horse and companion, all because she was too heavy, strained his heart, so she killed him. Can you see the bit in there I've added from my after-dinner routine?

I just think the poor horse was cursed in some way. I mean, it just had to be Gala, didn't it? Was it not bad enough that my dad played for Gala, and that my brothers would eventually captain Gala?

Somewhat ironically, too, my sister is married to a chap from Gala, Douglas Mundell. That's Mundell to most folk, pronounced 'Mundull', but because Kirsty's a PE teacher in Edinburgh and has always wanted to be considered posh, for her it's 'Mundelle' – with an 'e' on the end. Who is she kidding? In these parts, they are still the Mundells from Cloven!

Just to digress further, Dougie – who was embarrassed to tell his pals that Kirsty was a former shot-put champion – actually played rugby for Melrose. I say played in the loosest sense. His career highlights (appearing for the Thirds) included failing to stop the opposition winger from running in for a touchdown because Dougie was too busy chatting to folk pitch-side. Seriously.

His best, though, came, he says, against Duns, when he was so bored from not seeing the ball out on the wing that he decided to see if he could grab hold of the crossbar, as you do. No mean feat, it must be said, but somehow he managed to sprint and jump high enough to catch the bar. It did happen, because his stunt – which must have looked like something out of the film *Kes* – led to the Duns' winning try.

Unfortunately, Dougie caught the bar when facing away

from the pitch. A schoolboy error if you are ever planning on swinging from the crossbar during an actual game. Suddenly, there was a shout behind him and, looking around, Dougie could see some Duns players advancing. But, in jumping down, his legs cramped up and he couldn't move to prevent Duns scoring under the posts.

Where were camera phones when you most needed them?

As you have probably surmised, Kirsty and Dougie are well matched. But, for me, she is the person who denied me a potentially successful equestrian career, and forced me into rugby instead. I should thank her, but I prefer making her feel bad, even now.

Then again, perhaps it was a good job I took to the rugby field, otherwise not only would I have needed to listen to my dad telling me how good he was, but also my brothers, Thomas and Christopher, who like Faither, mostly played for Gala.

When Christopher appeared on the scene we were told he'd arrived in one of three ways.

One was that Mum had bought him off the shelf at M&S. This was entirely plausible. One minute she was in the food aisles, next thing she'd spotted a bargain boy. Two, it was either Christopher or a dog and, to be honest, it was more fun having him because he could walk himself. And thirdly, again entirely plausible, he was just a mistake. Out the three, I'd have settled for number two, but the alternative choice with a tail.

Because Christopher kept disappearing over the hills, looking for food, he turned into quite a tubby kid and answered to the nickname 'Chubbsy'. He says it was puppy fat, but I think he only said that to make me feel better about not getting a dog. He was the youngest, but the biggest.

I'd go and see him playing as a kid. I was never sure if him seeing his big brother was inspiring or intimidating. But it was nice to lend some support, especially when I knew he was never going to be as good as me.

On the other hand, I think it would be safe to say that Thomas and me have always had a love–hate relationship. That may be down to the fact he's a ginger and, because of that, hates everyone. Kirsty is also a ginger, as is Christopher. I'm just tall. Those Young Farmers . . .

There's not too many years between Thomas and me, so there was a bit of competition and rivalry. I never bullied him – that was the domain of Kirsty the shot-putter, and she dished it out to both me and Tam. My first recollection is of him running around the house, naked. He grew out of it eventually. He was thirteen or fourteen by then.

We used to do 'Superstars' – mega-assault courses with climbs, jumps and tunnels – over the hay bales when it was that time of year. We also had some great football matches – yes, you read that right – in the courtyard at the farm, when we had some of the farm workers and their kids all playing six-a-side matches. The old boy was a bit more flexible then and maybe that's where I developed the goalkeeping skills that meant I got to play amateur football for Stow in my late teens. That and the DNA from my grandfather, Bert. Actually, maybe better not get one of those DIY DNA tests. I might find out why I don't have ginger hair.

That we were able to play those games, and have a bit of

fun, only highlights the changes in farming today, and the numbers that the industry employed back then.

But football was only a pastime compared to the game we all participated in. Actually, being completely truthful, and Christopher would probably concur, Thomas was the best player out the three of us, by a measure. He just didn't seem to get the breaks and that's as important as ability in big-time sport, something I've mentioned elsewhere too.

Thomas and I played against each other on quite a few occasions. The first time he played for Gala against Melrose, he was on the wrong side of the ball at a ruck, and I pulled him out the way because he was going to get a shoeing. I couldn't let that happen to my brother, even in a Gala jersey. The same thing happened the following year – but this time he got a kicking. Me, first in. He won't do that again.

One of the last matches I played at the Greenyards was against Gala. We were trying to win the title, Gala were trying to avoid relegation. Thomas was quoted all over the newspapers: 'Weir going to be a family at war,' proclaimed *The Sun*, 'but only for eighty minutes.'

Really? What about the previous twenty years?

Thomas certainly talked up Gala's chances. But we won 31–11, won the Premier Division 1 and Gala went down. All talk.

Thomas and Christopher both ended up at Melrose, where they put the jersey on for a year. Notice I didn't say played.

There was, as I say, always a wee edge between me and Thomas. He'd get a bit uppity, I'd put him in his place, or at least try. One year, after the Royal Highland Show, Thomas was upset that I'd stayed on to buy the broadcaster Dougie Vipond, who I've worked a lot with over the years, a drink. It wasn't the drink that upset my brother, but that Dougie hadn't spoken to him when he came to film on the farm one time. How typically ginger.

He was still upset when we stopped at the chip shop on the way home. Thomas put all his change in his hand to count it out and I hit his hand and made him drop it all, and it rolled down the street. Back in the car, with Mother driving, Thomas noticed that I had a fish supper, my dad had a fish supper and our late brother-in-law, Michael Dun, had a fish supper, but because I'd lost him all his loose change, he only had chips. So he leaned across, over Michael who was in the middle, and punched me on the cheek. Naturally, I retaliated by giving him a slap back, still holding my fish and chips. Michael didn't help the situation, trying to give a commentary and then act as judge, while my old man, sitting in the front, broke off momentarily from his fish supper to shout, 'Take them to the police station.' Thankfully it didn't come to that, only because Mum wanted home.

Thomas has always been the fighter, and a bit tougher than me. When I did the filming for TV with John Beattie and Rona Dougall to launch my charity, Thomas sent me a text saying, 'Stop being such a fanny and grow up.' That was his caring nature shining through.

What was great, though in very sad circumstances, was that all three of the brothers did get to play together. We took part in a memorial rugby match six years ago for a policeman friend of ours, Steve Cully, who had been a good rugby player and a distance runner, who died suddenly aged just forty-one in September 2011.

Thomas, Christopher and me – although I was maybe not quite at my racing weight – played in a select team alongside Gregor Townsend, Scott Hastings, Peter Wright, Gary Armstrong, Barry Stewart and a few others, against a team of Lothian and Borders police officers. It was a terrific tribute to Steve and raised a few quid for Chest Heart & Stroke Scotland.

A special day – but playing with my brothers was something really special for me as well. And despite all the shenanigans, the horsing around and the jibes – ginger or otherwise – I couldn't have asked for better brothers, sister and family. Particularly now.

3

Melrose and the
Lean Years

THE TITLE OF THIS CHAPTER may be slightly misleading.
During my time playing for Melrose at the Greenyards
there were no lean years in terms of success, either as a team
or an individual. The leanness was entirely natural and to
do with my physique.

I wasn't quite as tall as I am now when I started playing
at Stewart's Melville, where, to be honest, I was seen as a
big lanky lad who could jump but wasn't very hard. At the
same time, Sandy Fairbairn, who was part of the Duke of
Buccleuch Pony Club, suggested I join the Melrose Under
14s team. It was a logical choice.

My dad and brothers, Thomas and Christopher, either
had or would play for Gala, but Gala held their mini and
junior sessions on a Saturday, which was when we were at
the pony club. Melrose, however, practised on a Sunday.

After fourth year at school, you went up against the fifth-
and sixth-year boys, and thankfully I went up in the world
as well by a few more inches, and toughened up a bit too,

enjoying the competitiveness and physical nature of the game. A natural forward then.

But rugby still wasn't high on my agenda, unlike equestrianism. My main love was horses, but I fell into, or grew into, rugby. I'll be totally honest: everything I achieved through rugby was an unexpected bonus.

That may sound somewhat blasé, but I am being truthful. I'd have been just as happy competing at the Horse of the Year Show, or the Hickstead Derby, or Gatcombe Park, or Burghley, as I would at Lansdowne Road or Parc des Princes, quite possibly happier. I'm not dismissing my achievements, and neither do I want to sound condescending by making out that rugby came easily to me. But in some ways it did.

I never had to work as hard as some did to get to the level I played at. Carl Hogg, for example, put so much in, and put a terrible toll on his body, but though he did play for Scotland, to my mind he never got the recognition his effort deserved. But you could say that about a lot of players, and a lot more about people in other lines of work.

I may have been tall, and strong with it, but I was extremely sinewy so carried little weight. This was one of the reasons why I could carry on my equestrian pursuits for so long: the horse could still carry me, comfortably, because by the time I started playing seriously for Melrose in my late teens, I was still only thirteen stone in weight.

At school I had been very shy and the rugby brought me out of my shell. You can't play a team sport and not communicate, you can't play a team game and not have your say, and you can't play rugby and not answer back when someone is having a go at you. I grew up quite quickly, playing for the Melrose Colts team. Actions often speak louder than words, yes, and especially on the rugby field. But sometimes you need a voice.

I inherited the number 8 position in the Firsts at the Greenyards when Carl Hogg – Hoggy – was absent through injury. When he came back, he should have been thrown in at lock, but instead brought a sick note from his mammy, which he gave to the coach, who happened to be his uncle Jim – one Jim Telfer. Is the word nepotism?

And so it was me who was shoved into the second row, hardly a prime specimen for that position. I tried desperately to bulk up. I ate handsomely, but never put any pounds on. Later I got into shakes, which were guaranteed to beef you up, but all I wanted to do was throw up. I didn't like them and neither did my body. No weight gained there either. I must have been the biggest lightweight heavyweight in Scottish rugby.

Later in my career, Alan Tomes and Alister Campbell, both second-rowers for Hawick and Grand Slam winners in 1984 (that was why I listened to them, not because they were from Hawick) told me I'd reach a certain age – although I might have to wait until my mid-twenties – and then put on a stone for no reason. I might have exceeded that by a few pounds, but they were right, although I still reckoned I was lighter than some of my counterparts.

However, with my mobility, I was equally adept at lock or on the back row. That dual role would be a useful asset when it came to gaining international honours. And like my progress with Melrose, any strides I made with Scotland were in no small measure thanks to Jim Telfer.

'Creamy' – as Jim was nicknamed – was a godsend to a young player. Perhaps I didn't identify that immediately. But he would coach you so you'd learn. And often you would learn because he made you work things out for yourself. So, inevitably, it would stick.

He was the coach you needed if you wanted to succeed. You might not like him or his methods, but ultimately you were going to go further listening to him – usually because he was screaming in your ear.

Jim was all about preparation, regardless of what team you were playing for. His team talks, which became speeches more often than not, were unforgettable. Many will be familiar with his 'Everest' speech on the 1997 Lions tour. No, he wasn't selling double glazing. But he'd picked on a theme to get his message across, and some of his thinking could be quite out the box.

Once, when we were with Scotland, he lined all the chairs up, two-by-two. This was the team bus, and Basil, being the captain, had to be in the driver's seat. We were giggling away and all you could see were the boys dropping their heads, shoulders bouncing up and down, trying our best not to laugh but failing miserably. Not in case we got a row, but because we wanted to see where the bus was going.

The point Jim was making was that we were all on-board together and going in the same direction. Then someone asked, 'Are we there yet?' and Jim went doolally.

There was another time down at Twickenham, when Jim didn't like the way we had got on the bus. I think the word he used was slovenly. I had to look it up, but Jim wasn't happy, oh no. So, he took us all off again and made us run around the bus, do some press-ups and then stuck us back on the coach. He wasn't pleased. We still lost. He wasn't pleased at that either.

And, from being someone who communicated brilliantly with the players to get his message over, but who maybe didn't have a great deal of time for the media or marketing part of the game, suddenly Jim turned into voice-over man, appearing on TV adverts and videos.

I could praise him to the hilt for different things, load up on the compliments and platitudes, but instead I will sum up everything rugby has been to me in a line. Without Jim Telfer, I wouldn't be sitting here writing a book about my career and life in rugby because I wouldn't have had one and no one would be that interested in me now.

Luck, fate, coincidence, call it what you will. But I was so fortunate that my time at Melrose ran parallel with the club having arguably Scotland's greatest ever coach, and a whole bunch of supremely talented players: Basil (Bryan Redpath), Chick (Craig Chalmers), Graham Shiel, Hoggy (Carl Hogg), Craig Joiner and Rowen Shepherd, all of whom I played with for Scotland, but there were other players key to that success too. Andrew 'Pansy' Kerr was one such player, but he kept disappearing to Norway to deliver sheep. Robbie Brown, my partner in the boiler room, was a real grafter, an absolute work horse, and Stevie 'Puddin' Brotherstone would eventually end up at the Falcons – and not forgetting Andrew 'Ripper' Redpath, who could play anywhere on the back row.

Five Scottish championship titles we won in seven seasons during my time at Melrose. Impressive consistency, but even that wasn't enough for some. Get beaten on a Saturday and you would have Eric the Red, a great Melrose stalwart, at the end of the bar in the Greenyards, telling you in no uncertain terms how useless he thought you were. It incentivised you to go out and prove him wrong, just so you would have something to come back at him with. But it could be the same in the baker's, or on the high street. Always someone with an opinion.

You don't get the opportunity to get above your station either. There is always someone to remind you of a pass you dropped, or a tackle you missed, how drunk you got, or where you fell asleep after a night on the pop.

Winning national titles was one thing, but in some folk's minds, there was a bigger prize to be had. The Borders and the clubs that made up the Border League at that time – Melrose, Gala, Hawick, Selkirk, Jed-Forest, Kelso and Langholm – were a real hotbed of talent and competition. You might have to beat Watsonians or Stirling County to gain national honours, but on occasion the toughest test you would face would be against those from your own backyard. Forget the points. The fight for bragging rights, be they for a week, a month, a year – or in the case of the rivalry within the Borders, for years after you've stopped playing – was intense.

It might not have had the status or cachet of, say, Warriors against Racing, or Edinburgh–Munster, but, trust me, an end-of-season game at Riverside Park against Jed, on one of those dreich, miserable nights where winter was still trying to upset spring, was every bit as committed and intense as anything you might face in the European Cup or PRO14. Trust me on that.

Take one step up from club rugby at Melrose and you were putting yourself in the frame for serious honours at international level. Naturally, the competition went up a notch too. You were never going to get in the Scotland team if you couldn't beat your direct opponents at a domestic level.

One such opponent was Stewart Campbell. Such a quiet guy, unassuming, the type who if you said we're not throwing the ball to you today, but all we want you to do is contest the opposition put-in – which could be a thankless job – would just get on with it. But Stewart would be one of my toughest opponents, hugely aggressive and disruptive. I always thought he was never credited for a lot of the work he did; and wrongly so, I have to say. But if you played next to him, or with him, you couldn't be anything else but impressed.

He also left an impression on me. Look closely at my lip and you will see a scar. That was him, playing for North & Midlands up in Dundee against the South, when he came from behind and stuck one on me. We're still good friends. I always mention it every time I see him, but we're still pals.

However, I was always more impressed with Stewart being able to play musical instruments. For someone who would struggle with a kazoo, I admired the coordination it took to get a tune out of something. How do you learn the guitar? I suppose buying one would be a start.

He has also been such a joy of late, helping me and the Foundation: another star.

But back to Melrose, and of all the silverware I got to lift at the Greenyards, one piece stands out.

One of the biggest thrills for me was winning the Melrose Sevens, not with Melrose, but with the Co-Optimists select team, featuring the likes of Andy Nicol, Derek Turnbull and Gregor Townsend in 1993. Playing for Melrose, and with the Sevens invented by local butcher Ned Haig away back in 1883, I knew the importance and significance to the club of the Sevens tournament and the kudos that came with being a winner. I just don't think some appreciated me taking away a winner's medal when it hadn't been Melrose who had won.

The Ladies Cup is not a very big trophy, but it means so much to those brought up with the history and heritage of Sevens, and it was great to collect a winner's medal. Carl Hogg also won the tournament; he says he is a three-time winner, but the year I recall most was when he had the cheek to collect a medal even though he was just a reserve.

I enjoyed Sevens, and a good few experts reckoned I was pretty decent at it, being strong, lanky, a good jumper and, once I got into my stride, quite quick. Unfortunately, there might not have been the same emphasis on Sevens rugby, nationally, as there is today. Shame that.

I'd have fancied playing in the Olympics or the Commonwealth Games. Or maybe it was the globetrotting the players do now – to Hong Kong, Dubai, Singapore and Las Vegas – that would have appealed more. Those places would probably have just edged out Stirling County and GHK as attractive destinations.

4

My First Cap

I WAS DOING THE BUSINESS with Melrose, but I think my promotion to the full squad was considered to have been somewhat accelerated, which surprised a few people – let's call them the traditionalists – and even me up to a point.

I'd been involved in the Scottish Schools team when I was at Stewart's Melville, that would have been in 1988, and I went to New Zealand with them. Earlier that season, I'd played alongside Andy Nicol, Steve Brotherstone, Scott Nichol and Dan Pulfrey against my English counterparts at Clarkston, and had my first encounter with an equally young Martin Johnson, who was joined by Damian Hopley, Adedayo Adebayo, Steve Ojomoh and Paul Challinor.

The most memorable – or maybe forgettable – part of that tour was when me and Richie Gray (that's the Gala Richie Gray if you are trying to do the arithmetic), were told by Rob Moffat, who was the coach, that if we ever played like that again we'd be sent home.

Did I think that was a possibility – or a threat that could be carried out? Not really. You'd have needed to do something pretty serious to be sent home from a Schools tour, and, to be honest, if it was that bad the New Zealand constabulary would probably have been wanting a few words first.

I know coaches sometimes say things in the heat of the moment, but that threat is something I laugh at now. I think it took me and Richie all our energy not to start giggling when we were being given that dressing down.

But we survived because, joking aside, it incentivised us to pull the finger out. I think you realise then that representative rugby, at any level, carries responsibilities. It's not like school or your club, when after a day you are back to normal and training and playing. In the representative game, any misdemeanour or poor display might not be considered for several weeks, by which time the people in charge have played out umpteen scenarios in their head and decided you are not for them. So, lesson learned.

The next time I went on tour to New Zealand was two years later – with the full Scotland squad.

You have to remember that Scotland had just won the 1990 Grand Slam that year and, for some, changing a winning team or introducing new faces was maybe a bit risky. But Ian McGeechan, the coach, obviously had an eye to the future. Graham Shiel, another of the Melrose boys, was, like me, uncapped, and also called up to travel.

I was still only nineteen, utterly raw in this kind of company, and the pair of us came in watching this well-oiled machine in action every day – in training, on the plane, around the dining room, on the bus. It was, to be honest, an eye opener. It always is, when you move up a level, from school to club rugby, from there to the district game.

But, as wee laddies, so to speak, this was being taken out of your comfort zone, suddenly asked to grow up really quickly in that environment. I think we did that, but you would see or come across others in future years, young players tipped for the top, who didn't manage that leap and were left behind. That is just the brutal reality of top-level sport.

It was, however, great fun, and a bit of an adventure. The make-up of rugby then was exciting because, as a kid, you could see yourself playing for Scotland, everyone could. Then you learned that if you used the talent you had, and did certain things, like perform well, and do what was asked, there was a route that would take you to the higher echelons of the sport. It was the ladder effect, but you could step on to that ladder at any age, and from many different backgrounds. I just wonder if rugby these days, in general, offers up that same pathway, because from the outside it looks like if you don't make it into an academy set-up, then you're not quoted. But I could be wrong. I have been before – just the once, mind.

Anyway, New Zealand was a great experience. David Sole was our captain, and I was with the team I had watched beating England on St Patrick's Day – from the schoolboy terracing at Murrayfield. I think I got in because of my boyish good looks.

But what a difference in two years and two tours, from the Schools trip to the Full Monty.

In 1988, on the Schools tour, we were handed badges to sew on to our blazers and had to fund a lot of it ourselves. We also stayed in 'billets', where families in different places would have boys lodging with them. That was a very nice experience, because you saw what people you'd never seen or met before were willing to do for you, all because you had a bit of talent for chasing an egg, and they could relate to that. That gesture, that kindness, is just so typical of rugby. Today, thirty years on, I'm experiencing it daily. And when I was in New York in early 2018, I even met up with some of the people who put me up on that 1988 trip. I couldn't have been that bad a boarder!

But having learned to sew just to look part of a team, when I went to New Zealand in 1990 things were a bit different: travelling business class, only turning left when you boarded long-haul flights, being handed blazers and ties and flannels. And we trained at the Old Course Hotel in St Andrews before the tour.

Dunky Paterson was the tour manager, and the man with the credit card, and in what would be described as a bonding session, he invited a mix of the boys – me being one of them – up to the bar for a wee whisky. Not any whisky, mind you: a Glen Grant, 1936, at £130 a dram. So, I had two of them. I then had a Famous Grouse, keeping in with our sponsors around that time – and I couldn't tell the difference between that and the Glen Grant. I wasn't really a whisky drinker then. I might do a bit better now.

But it was a very nice gesture from Dunky, even if he was from Gala.

It all went towards making you feel part of the team – and what a team – the best side in the Northern Hemisphere. Anyone thinking otherwise, look at the history books. Despite our status, I still think the All Blacks had more to lose than us, playing in their own backyard, and as the best team in the world.

I don't think there is a better way of getting to know your teammates than on a tour, especially one so far away. I knew some of the players, the Melrose boys: Shiely, as I say, and Chick (Craig Chalmers), who was the starting 10, in with the bricks already. Chick could enjoy himself, but he was a dedicated trainer, and you knew how seriously he took things. You'd hear the speedball going most days, always at it.

There were others, though I only knew them through playing against them in the League or Border League, or in the District Championship. I knew of them and respected them as great players. But even having played for South, for instance, you would pretty much go your own way and do your own thing, which meant heading back to the Greenyards. I'd never really socialised with any of the boys from Kelso, Hawick or Selkirk, or spent time in their company. I was still quite young for a start, and I was still making my road in the game. Touring changes all that.

While I'd trained with these guys at Gleneagles ahead of the 1990 Five Nations, now you were rubbing shoulders with them daily: JJ (John Jeffrey), Finlay (Calder), wee Gaz (Armstrong). These guys, though none of them made anything of it, had taken on legendary status after winning that Grand Slam. It didn't make them any different – although these days they always have it in their locker to put someone's gas at a peep – but, as a teenager on that trip in such exalted company, it did have you pinching yourself on occasions.

Again, it was such a big adventure. But you had to

believe that you were good enough to be in their company. Confidence in my ability – I don't think I ever struggled with that. But I can see why individuals coming into a team, and a very successful team in the case of Scotland in 1990, could be overawed and go into their shell. I suppose that how you handle those kinds of things becomes just as important as natural skill and ability as you step up.

Some of the senior players did their own thing. You couldn't just walk in and gatecrash that hierarchy. As Scotland teammates they'd been at it for a while, seen it, done it. You were one of the minions and still had to earn your wings. And you did, if you did your job and performed, and avoided threats of being sent home.

Being with Scotland on tour, seriously, as a teenager this was living the dream, even if I was one of 'Brewster's Beezers', which was the Wednesday team with Alex Brewster, the Stew Mel prop, in charge of us. I'll watch what I say here. I think what I'm trying to put over is covered by the phrase 'baptism of fire'.

The games were taken very seriously. We were in New Zealand. Everything rugby orientated is serious. But there was a different dynamic to the midweek team, which brought some experienced and very good players together alongside us boys and the less established names. We did go out to win, but also to enjoy ourselves in the process.

That was the tour where one of the commentators said, 'Dougie Wyllie goes for the gap that only he can see . . .' which was very funny. But while we had a great time, the midweek guys never lost. Indeed, apart from the two Tests against the world champions, in Dunedin and Auckland,

Scotland went unbeaten throughout that trip, the first time it had happened on a Southern Hemisphere tour. It was good to have played a part in achieving that feat.

I weighed about thirteen stone, wet, when I went on that tour. So, when I played, I made sure I was scrummaging behind Iain Milne – 'The Bear' – as he was a good bit healthier than me and had always finished his pudding, and boy could he hold a corner up himself. A colossal player, and, for a big guy, quick and good with his hands. I don't think he noticed whether I was pushing behind him or not. I was there to keep him company, let's say.

But Bear was a huge help on that tour, a great talker, as was Alex (Brewster), and Chris Gray, who adopted me to be his little boy. I was the apprentice, and these boys took me under their wing, gave me some guidance, fatherly advice, call it what you will, even though in the case of Chris, I was going to be directly vying for his place in the team.

I think it takes a really unselfish attitude to do that and it's a classic and classy example of being a real team player. It taught me a lot and I'd like to think that as I went from being a laddie to a senior player, both at club level and international, I gave some of that back.

Looking back, you realise just how many people were on your side and wanted you to succeed. That doesn't always happen in life.

After the tour to New Zealand, it was like having to start all over again. Just because you'd gone out with the big boys for the summer jaunt didn't mean anything for the next season. What I'd learned, I had to put back into action again.

Come time for the Autumn Test against Argentina, I

knew I was in with a shout of playing against them and when Damian Cronin was injured, I was drafted in for my first cap on the 10th of November 1990 at Murrayfield.

It's a date I'll never forget.

It was a great honour and meant all those dreams you'd had of playing for your country as a kid had become a reality. However, being honest, I don't know if the game was as big a thrill as getting the call-up in the first place.

We won convincingly, by forty-odd points, and Chris Gray scored a try, just to keep me in my place. The only other memory I have of that game was before the kick-off. I came out the tunnel behind Gary Armstrong, and as we waited for the anthems, Gary gave me a nudge. I thought he was going to pass on some inspirational thoughts to put some fire in the belly. Instead, all he wanted to ask is whether I had seen that particularly well-endowed girl beside the Royal Box. Such insight, such focus!

After I'd played in my first game, and we'd beaten the Pumas, Paul Burnell gave me his jersey, so that when we swapped shirts, I didn't have to give away my first Scotland shirt. A great gesture, and something I did a few times myself over the years – probably why I don't have too many old Scotland shirts of my own. But it is the kind of thing that goes on, among teammates and men who become really great comrades and friends, unbeknown to the wider public.

But international rugby, international sport, is also very much a dog-eat-dog environment. There is a time and a place for friendships, but having won one cap, the aim was most certainly to win a few more. I had quite enjoyed it.

★

Even me, big stupid from the Borders, knew that 1991 was a massive year for Scottish rugby. Firstly, that we'd be asked to defend the Grand Slam and the Five Nations Championship, and that we'd then end the year with the World Cup.

As I explained, playing for Scotland had been top of my agenda. However, without sounding condescending, and it might do to those who never had the privilege to play for their country, getting that first cap was easy. Once you get to a certain level or standard, you are almost guaranteed a cap. Why? Because coaches and selectors want to see you at the next level, and want to test you, even if that means breaking you. That box had been ticked by all parties in the Argentina game. Now, staying in the Scotland team became the focus, doubly challenging and doubly difficult.

I'd heard it said about other sports, and champions in boxing or tennis or Formula 1, or whatever, that becoming Number 1 was hard but staying there was harder. Stephen Hendry, the great snooker champion, won many titles and was champion of the world seven times. But for him, being the top dog, the Number 1 in his sport for many years, was what mattered to him most. It showed consistency, it showed that over the piece you were better than your contemporaries. I was going to make sure I gave myself every chance of keeping my place in that Scotland team.

You've sampled that success, and now you have a goal and a target. You also have a target on you, because those in possession of those jerseys won't give them up easily. Other players want to take away your opportunity.

Strangely, and again this depends so much on how you handle the psychology around it, it isn't the guys from England, or France, or Argentina, or wherever, that can do your international prospects the least amount of good. No, those who can do you untold damage are the guys who are your squad colleagues, maybe even – as I would find out at Newcastle – your very club teammates. The guys who you train with and who you could be selected for the international squad with, they're the ones who can ultimately take your place in the team.

Winner takes all; dog eats dog. International rugby is about competition, from when you claim your peg in the dressing room until the final whistle sounds. At times that is tough, and I wonder how many who watch sport actually get that part of it?

I was fortunate. The coaches liked what they saw and selected me for the Argentina game. But by the time the Five Nations came around in early 1991, the start of the big year I mentioned, I was out the team.

Surely some mistake? Actually, no.

The trial game, Blues versus Reds, finished 10–10. It was a horrible day where the wind made line-out throws a lottery. Chris Gray was a sure-fire starter, and the other place would be between me and Damian Cronin, and he got the nod.

Kicking off the 1991 Five Nations as holders, I think Ian McGeechan, as coach, decided to go with the guys who had delivered the big prize the previous year. Understandable, and that was how I reconciled myself to the fact that I hadn't kept my place in the Scotland team. That, and the thought that while I believed I was playing well, maybe others had been playing better, or I just didn't show enough in that trial. I'd need to improve, play better, and make sure I couldn't be ignored.

Later on, and after establishing myself in the Scotland team, my thinking changed: I was deserving of the place, and those who kept trying to take it maybe weren't quite as good. A degree in self-taught sports psychology – all the best sportsmen and women have one.

Having sat out the entire Five Nations, thankfully I was back in the frame for the World Cup. But after that, oh the agonies of waiting to see if you'd been selected for an international or a tour! No texts or messaging apps back then. It was the good old-fashioned postie for us, although for my first cap against the Pumas, the letter was hand-delivered by Dunky Paterson. Maybe it's not true what they say about Gala folk. But most of the time, it was all about waiting on that wee red van making an appearance. And if you lived on a farm in the Borders, sometimes the wider public would know before you did.

When the mail did arrive on time, even then, a glance at the envelope would tell you if it was good news and you were playing, or bad news and you were just in the squad. You didn't get a letter to say thanks but no thanks.

Bill Hogg, the secretary of the Scottish Rugby Union, had a wee system whereby he'd write your team number on the envelope, so the letters would correspond with the envelopes. See a 4, or a 5, or an 8 – happy days! See a number in the teens, throw it on the fire. You were a bench-warmer. Unless they'd mistaken you as a back. Possible, given some of the places I'd turn up occasionally.

Actually, as my career progressed, Ceefax and Teletext became the source of good or bad news – what was it, page 371 on Ceefax – because invariably the press would get news of the team before our post arrived on the farm. I remember those heart-in-mouth moments as the page on the telly would update, and there it was – still nothing!

Amazing how long you could watch the same page, sitting there, waiting for it to suddenly come up with a headline about who was making their debut or had been dropped.

Even if it wasn't for the lack of trying sometimes, thankfully that didn't happen too often over the next ten years.

5

Meet the Wife
and Family

MUCH OF MY JOURNEY HAS BEEN completed alongside my very capable co-pilot and wife, Kathy. I say co-pilot because she has steered me in a different direction on several occasions, maybe away from impending disaster, and kept us on an even and safe course thereafter. Now, you don't get a recommendation much better than that, do you?

I met Mary Doll – my pet name for Kathy in honour of Rab C. Nesbitt's beautiful and charming wife – for the first time when I was eighteen, at the Mosshouses point-to-point, as the two of us were into our horses in a big way. We already knew of the Hutchinson girls, all four of them, lovely but wild, and Kathy's sister married my dad's next-door neighbour, Michael Dun at Gilston – are you keeping up with this? I know it sounds like a plot from *Emmerdale*.

I'll say now, I did take a wee shine to her – I saw more potential in her than she did me (some things never change), but nothing then happened for a few years, although I did send her a postcard from every tour I was on. She asked me if I knew Gavin Hastings just before I set out on a Scottish tour to New Zealand, and of course I said I did, because I'd read his articles in the paper. That was in fact the only way I knew him at that time.

But Kathy wanted a postcard from Gavin, and I wasn't going to disappoint, and so I managed to get one from him and sent it to Kathy, all the way from New Zealand. It may have looked like my handwriting, but that was entirely coincidental.

While Kathy and I knew each other and had kept in touch, in a fashion, it was only after the two of us — and by now we were in our mid-twenties — had finished other relationships we'd been in that we got together. I was wondering what to do with myself, and decided to give Kathy a call and see what she was up to. As luck would have it, her mum and dad were away and she didn't have anything in for tea. Seizing the opportunity — and without so much of a hint of desperation in my voice — I asked if she'd like to go for something to eat and arranged to meet her halfway, at Buccleuch, fifteen minutes for me, fifteen minutes to around an hour-plus for her.

She asked her sister Gina what she should do. Thankfully Gina said the right thing — that Kathy had nothing in for tea so she might as well go, and if nothing came of it, at least she would get fed. That was the beginning of a beautiful relationship and we haven't stopped eating since.

A turning point came when the Scottish Rugby Union decided they were going to allow — and pay for — WAGs to go on the trip to South Africa for the World Cup in 1995.

Kathy wasn't sure. I sold it – again with no hint of desperation – by saying that if it didn't work out at least she'd get a holiday out of it. I still think that was the only reason she went.

We married a couple of years later when I came back from the Lions tour to South Africa in 1997. The wedding date had been planned before I got the call from the Lions, which fortunately, I mean unfortunately, meant Kathy was left to do much of the wedding planning herself. When I was injured on that tour, I came back with a revised guest list of who I maybe wanted to invite, gave it to her, then after a couple of days, went back to South Africa.

She appeared to have everything in hand, and I would just have got in the way. Even now, it seems a completely plausible alibi. I did organise two things. One was the wedding car, and for that Sir John Hall allowed me to borrow his Bentley, with the NUFC number plate. Very nice.

As was my second contribution, the honeymoon in Mauritius. I had some style, although this was ahead of what must have been a culture shock for Mary Doll. Actually, I think on that trip it was dawning on her what the future may hold.

While I'd lived at her parents home for a bit, we'd never lived together. I think those first few months after the wedding were a struggle for Kathy to accept my way of living as a professional rugby player. I say few months, probably until I retired actually. Make that up until the present.

For three years we led a typical, some would say chaotic, lifestyle. We lived life to the full and enjoyed ourselves, all with the backdrop of me having to be a professional athlete.

Maybe after those three years we decided that it was time to calm down and play at being real grown-ups.

I don't think much planning went in to us starting a family, or any kind of biological clock ticking. It seemed a good idea and so it has proved. What I'd noticed, being the social voyeur that I am, was how the gaps between kids – if you decide to have them at all – can have an effect on what you do as a family. I knew this from my own family life, growing up. I'd also seen people I knew struggle around holidays, childcare and the likes, when they had, say, a ten- and a five-year-old as well as a toddler or baby.

Instead, we had ours in a batch. Someone likened it to me growing up on a farm and believing there was a season for children as there was for lambs. Not so, but actually . . .

Hamish was first to arrive, in December 2000, between Christmas and New Year. I don't think I remember much of either. Angus came along in April 2002, then Ben in February 2004. Would we have wanted a girl? Maybe, if things had worked out differently, but by the time Ben arrived I was planning a future away from rugby. What that means is our niece Charlotte has become something of an adopted daughter, and we've been there at her twenty-first, graduation and the likes.

Three boys it was for us, two born in England, with Ben a Scot by birth. I wanted them all born in Scotland, but because of logistics and practical reasons, it didn't happen. In other words, Kathy said no. Still, one disagreement in twenty-one years of wedded bliss isn't bad.

Remember that social voyeurism I mentioned, and how teenagers might not want to go places or on holiday with a toddler? One in the pub and one in the crèche. You get the picture. This thought was, of course, completely ignoring the complexities of having three kids within a three-year age range. Which meant that you needed and got everything times three. The back seats of cars were wiped out by child seats, and that also meant that at any one time there might have been two buggies on the go, and one being carried. Hardly meticulous planning.

You also ended up with three times the bills, illnesses (as one passed on their spots, sniffs and sickness to another), and if one cried at least one other would come out in sympathy. Then there was the fighting, when the house regularly looked as if you'd walked in on a WWE Super Show-Down, except with three times the noise.

Your parenting skills also changed rather quickly, as did your sleep patterns. For instance, anything belonging to Hamish that was dropped or needed washed was thrown in the washing machine or sterilised immediately. Angus would have his run under a tap, while Ben would have his licked clean or turned outside in and then be sent on his way. Of the three, Ben probably has an immune system second to none.

On holiday, or of a weekend (depending on matches), you might have a late one, a three or four in the morning shot. The kids would see daylight and could be up at five or six. How on earth did we survive?

Well, somehow, we did survive what might be called those demanding years, and now the only demands being made are for hard cash.

Still, what it did mean was some incredibly cute (they'll

love me for using that word) photographs of the three of them through the years, from babies all the way up until the present. It seems no time at all since I plonked Hamish inside the Tetley Bitter Cup when the Falcons won it, or there's that photo of the three of them being on their best behaviour on the back seat.

Now look at them. Three handsome young men – some of their better features may have come from their mother, I'll admit – and a trio we are really proud to call ours. They are our salt, our rocks.

6

Christmas 2016

CHRISTMAS 2016 WAS NEVER going to be straightforward, even before we'd been given the news about MND. My mum was seriously ill, suffering from cancer, and given not a long time to live. She's still here as well. Us Weirs are made of tough stuff. Well, Mother is.

With Mum's circumstances in mind, it wasn't really the time to tell anyone, especially the family, about my news. Simply put, we decided to get Christmas and New Year out the way first. No point in spoiling people's festivities and parties.

Did I feel like partying? No, not really. But the party was on and we would party on. MND, or anything else for that matter, wasn't going to break a habit of a lifetime.

Almost from day one, we had to put a brave face on things. It was made slightly easier with our mum being rushed into hospital on Christmas Eve. I say easier but, of course, it wasn't. We all had serious concerns about Mum, but, in some ways, you were able to hide behind those emotions, and people would take your mood or upset as being how you were feeling about her, rather than anything that might be going on in your own life.

But it was a tricky time. I say this as a master of understatement.

Like so many families, Christmas is a huge part of the year, as are, say, summer holidays. It quickly dawns on you, however, how important every day is: there was no avoiding it. It was quite possible that this could be my last Christmas, our last Christmas. Anyone who has children will know how much they mean to them. And here was me and Kathy knowing something that our children were blissfully unaware of. At some point, and soon, they would have to know. Christmas just wasn't the time for it, especially if it could be our last one together. Or was it the right time, so we could make something of it? That question typifies the decision and thought processes you go through, time and time again, having been diagnosed with MND. I suppose it's the same with any serious or terminal condition.

But me and Kathy had decided the course of action and we were going to stick to it, regardless of how difficult it was to look at Hamish, Angus and Ben, so totally oblivious to the turmoil that was going on in my head and, I don't mind saying, in my heart.

That emotional rollercoaster is simply something you need to overcome. You either get used to the highs and lows, or you will fall off. There isn't any coaching book, or crib sheet, or online service that tells you how to cope with your brain throwing out more scenarios and permutations than a lottery machine, or what to do when your heart feels as if it's stuck in your throat.

You learn to cope better and, almost, put up a defensive shield. I've been quite adept at that. Maybe I should become a poker player.

A lot of the time, though, in public it will come across as me being myself. Actually, it's me taking control of a situation, at an event, during an interview. I know what's coming next and I don't want to go there. Attack becomes the best form of defence. And folk just think it's me trying to be funny. Which I am. But there is a serious element to it, too.

That doesn't stop you being blindsided on occasions when something comes at you from left field. You need to have your wits about you. Occasionally, it's impossible not to become emotional.

That festive weekend was a very steep learning curve for both me and Kathy. The family Christmas was going to be at my sister's house. Mum had wanted to have everyone gathered around her and Dad, because it could have been her last Christmas. However, given how she was, it would have been too much for her, hence why the Mundells became our hosts, and a jolly fine spread and party they put on. It was so good, I actually forgot what I'd been told on the Friday. Then it came back to me with a jolt. But, whether I'd thought about it or not previously, I was suddenly acutely aware that Mum had been enduring the same emotions as I was starting to go through. God, she must be constructed of hard stuff.

Perhaps that Christmas was a good time to learn. As I said, the reality that it could be your last Christmas was one thing. But, through time, you realise how many things could be your last.

You might want to do something different for Christmas next year, or go somewhere different on holiday, celebrate a birthday or anniversary at a certain place, or visit a restaurant, a friend, even the dentist or bank (neither particularly pleasurable, so why I said that, I'm not sure). But, you get my point. Basically, as a rule, you are pretty positive there will be another time, another visit, another chance to do something. That is not a luxury afforded you by MND.

That Christmas – I refer to it as 'that Christmas' as I would be unlucky to have another one like it – was one where no one knew anything, not even me. Would I be walking for the next one, or in a wheelchair, or even still here? Trust me, two out of those three ain't bad.

My outlook – and maybe one it would benefit everyone to have – is live for today, and tomorrow is a bonus. It certainly was a bonus seeing another Christmas in 2017, and being able to celebrate it normally. I say normally, but I enjoyed it as much as I have any Christmas or festive period. It was an opportunity I'd hoped for, and I wasn't going to let it slip past quietly. I was still walking and talking, and Mum, despite some ups and downs, was still here.

And the boys? They maybe thought all their Christmases had arrived at once. Nothing was off Santa's radar, and they pretty much got everything they wanted. 'Yes' was the stock answer to the question, 'Could I please have?'

Expensive, yes. But what the hell, it's only money. Hopefully it will be expensive next Christmas as well. Trust me, it's worth paying for.

7

New Year, Same Fear

CHRISTMAS AND NEW YEAR were over in a flash. We had managed to get through them, one way or another, which was not easy. Now people – and by that I mean those closest to me, my immediate family – had to be told. And, given how Mum was, that was never going to be simple. In fact, the word simple was being slowly dropped from my vocabulary. Parents, kids, siblings. This hammer blow, this bombshell, this time bomb was something none of them had expected. Why would they? I'd complained about aches and pains for the last thirty years. Why would they take any notice of me having something wrong with my hand? Except it was anything but just a problem with my hand. It goes without saying, it was an emotional time.

'Incurable' is a word that seems to stun folk, and takes a while to sink in. Incurable, fatal, life ending. They were never very nice words to hear anyway. But now they applied to me, to those around me.

There is never an easy way to break such news. I couldn't find help with that on the internet. Needless to say, it was a conversation stopper. There was silence, a silence I broke because others were struggling to say much. There were also a few tears, hugs, words of comfort and support. There were even more of those once they'd typed 'MND' into their search engine.

With cancer, many people have experienced it, or know of someone with it, or have seen people die or survive, thanks to the wonderful drugs and treatment available to sufferers. Yes, it's not great news and you immediately fear the worst, but equally you know there might be a way of escaping it, a cure. When you break down MND, it's a bit more straightforward to cover some of the bases. One drug, no known cure, no guidelines on life expectancy. Simple facts, but not so comprehensible.

People have heard of MND without really knowing much in the way of detail about it. The rarity of the condition probably has a lot to do with that: in Scotland there are just over five hundred sufferers at any one time. Needless to say, there were still countless questions, but I wasn't really in a position to answer them all, given how little information I'd been given from the experts during my sit down with them. My family were hugely supportive, and they even started being nice to me for once, which was terribly off-putting because I had to be nice back to them. Still, it didn't take long before my brother, Thomas, was back to being himself, calling me a 'knob-end', which did give me some sort of normality. Seeking that normality was important to me. I wasn't going to change being who I am because of MND. But I didn't want others to change their attitude towards me either, which was why, in those early days (as I will explain), I only shared my news with those who I knew would treat me exactly the same, whether I had MND or a BMW. In either instance, I was probably going to get some flak.

However, in terms of my immediate family – and other friends later – the question they asked most in those early days was a virtual rewind and repeat of what I'd asked on that first day in Edinburgh, namely, 'How long have you got?' If only I knew, it might have been easier. But there was no easy answer. And that was the hardest part. Did I have a month, six months, a year, five years? I didn't know, so I couldn't tell them, and that is a terrible position to be in, especially when those nearest to you, your loved ones, are themselves looking for a bit of hope or positivity.

I didn't – and still don't – know what the timescale will be. But, from the outset, it was about setting targets, getting to experience them, and then setting more. I have to say, that is pretty much how I'd lived life anyway up to this news being delivered.

I don't know if people contemplate death or how they'd like to bow out. Some would want it to be quick; others would want to know how long they have. I'm definitely in the latter camp and always have been, and not just since my diagnosis. I say I'm comfortable with that, except I don't know how or when that eventual outcome will arrive.

If people have asked me questions, as I have asked others, then one I haven't given any thought to is, 'Why me?' Never. MND doesn't seem to happen through lifestyle or playing sport, being a farmer or a fisherman, a salesman or a postman. It is a completely random condition. 'Why me?'

is as impossible to answer as 'Why anyone?' – so why even contemplate it.

Others are believers, but I am not a greatly religious individual. About twenty years ago, I had a really bad car accident. I rolled my Land Rover Discovery, only about five hundred yards from my house. I'd been a wee bit silly. It was a very icy road, but if you followed the track, generally, you'd be fine. Except I got a wheel into a rut, and when the slush and snow sprayed up onto the windscreen, I never had a chance to put the wipers on, then *wham*. I drove off the road and off a hill, which flipped the car over a few times. You easily lose count when the only thing you are thinking about is when will this stop, and whether you will know when it has stopped. It was quite an impact. The headrest was sticking through the roof, the driver's door was ten yards away, and every panel was bent beyond repair. A right mess.

Surveying the damage to me and to the vehicle, I knew I'd been lucky. I was in a wee bit of a mess as well, rather shaken up, though relatively uninjured, and upside down. My hip had wedged under the steering wheel, but my legs were dangling out of the space where my door had been. Others will have had lesser impacts and been a lot less fortunate.

Now, that could have ended totally differently, a much worse outcome. I wondered a few times what the outcome might have been had someone else been in the car, as a passenger, rather than just me on my own. But, on that particular day, him upstairs might have been looking for a rugby player, but spared me because he was needing a proper number 8 and decided he didn't need to call me up just yet. Someone else would have been selected, someone less fortunate, and it could have happened to a builder, a farmer, a nurse, a lorry driver. But that day I got away with a fright, just a bit of a scare.

I say this in a way because my brother-in-law, Michael Dun, a farmer, at just fifty-four, wasn't so lucky. The fella upstairs decided one day he needed a shepherd. 'Dodgy Weir, I've seen you with sheep and actually you're not very good. Michael, he knows what he's doing, and so *You are coming with me, pal*' – and poor Michael was gone.

He got up one night, went to the bathroom and that was him, gone.

So, maybe this time around, the big chap in the sky has decided, 'Right, Weir, we've let you off a few times now, maybe you'd be quite good at handling this MND thing, so let's see what you can do.' If it wasn't me, it would have been someone else. And it has been, and will continue to be, when it comes to Motor Neurone Disease.

I know not everyone will see it that way, but that's how I see it. And, to be honest, my attitude, my philosophy if you want, towards everything has always been as simple as that.

People have asked if I'm upset. I am. I don't think that will change. But personally, when I look at everything George Wilson Weir has done in life, being blessed by being born into a great family, meeting Kathy and starting a family of my own, and the rugby, it hasn't been a bad forty-eight and a bit years, has it?

I'd still like a good few more, but compared to the hand others have been dealt, I've had a few aces along the way, whether it was drinking vintage whisky, or travelling first-class around the world, or being flown places in private jets, rubbing shoulders with the rich and famous – and that's just in Kelso – or the camaraderie of going on tour, the fabulous hotels you stay in, making lifelong friends in rugby, in business, in media, going places, seeing things, like being on safari in South Africa or being flown to Lapland and getting to meet Santa for BBC's *A Question of Sport* and, quite possibly above all else now, the response my illness has generated among people I've never met. All of that is quite marvellous. And I wouldn't change any of it.

The next phase, the next chapter, however, isn't so much about me. From here on in, it's about my family. Going forward, and that is the only direction we're headed, I will need them more than anything.

8

Joost van der Westhuizen

JOOST VAN DER WESTHUIZEN. From a rival who almost single-handedly ended my career as an international number 8, to a standard-bearer in the fight against Motor Neurone Disease and, eventually, a victim of this cruel condition. I have often thought about how, having played against him at Test level, I would then get to meet him again five years ago, at Murrayfield in 2013, both of us completely unaware of how we would eventually be linked by coincidence and circumstance.

In November 1994, I had been selected to face South Africa in Edinburgh, an Autumn Test between the two nations, and the first of two the Springboks would play.

They arrived, having started building a bit of a reputation for themselves as a very effective team, with a very good pack, and a very offence-orientated back division. Of course, a year later, names like van der Westhuizen, Francois Pienaar, Os du Randt, André Joubert and Mark Andrews would take on legendary status having won the third World

Cup, on their own patch, and in what was now a very new South African political landscape.

But that afternoon at Murrayfield, the Springboks gave us a taster of what to expect and, if truth be told, it wasn't exactly palatable for me, much of that thanks to Joost.

In the first half, from a scrum on the 22, he picked up and spun down the narrow-side, leaving me chasing him as he slid in for his first try. I got close, but not close enough. I should lodge my defence at this point – which is maybe more than I did on the day. But Dave McIvor was the blind-side flanker, and so the number 9 really was his man. He really was. Ask anyone. Dave even stayed attached to the scrum so it would make me look bad. That's my excuse, and I'm sticking to it.

A few minutes after the turnaround, he did it again, this time running straight through – or it might have been over – a ruck just outside our 22, avoiding several tackles and leaving our defence, including me again, in his wake. Our scrum-half, Derrick Patterson, should have been marking him. Ask anyone, except Dave McIvor.

Joost was unstoppable that day, and he knew it; he was acting like the big shot. He did have a bit of an attitude to him, arrogant almost, elbowing you, preferring to walk through you rather than around you and happy to make contact with you, even when the ball was dead. That was just his way, being confrontational, a bully, albeit a talented one. But I'd had enough of his antics.

So, in my best Afrikaans, I said something rather unprintable about him and his mother, and maybe even the sister he didn't have. In my experience, if you learn any phrases in another language, they tend to be things that are not nice, maybe even inflammatory, that will rile and get under the skin of an opponent.

My accent and pronunciation must have been passable, because he acknowledged what I'd said, tipping his head to the side, turning his mouth downward as if to say 'is that right?', and that was an end to his nonsense. Unfortunately, I'd left it until ten minutes from time before I said anything. If I'd been wiser, and maybe braver, I'd have said it sooner. Who knows, I could still have been a number 8. But Joost was a different guy thereafter.

He'd proved that day just how combative he was, one to watch, and on a personal level, put an end to me in the back row for evermore. I did tell him that a few years later, and that he'd ended mine and Gary Armstrong's talent-spotting competitions during the national anthems, as we'd never stand together again before matches – whereas previously, Gary and me would be picking out attractive young ladies in the stands. Honestly, it was just a way of calming the nerves. Still . . .

Four years later, in 1998, I would play against Joost again in another Autumn Test at Murrayfield, with an almost identical outcome in the Boks' favour, except I was at lock and blameless for any cock-ups in the fringe defence. Joost bagged a try. A year on, I came off the bench against the defending world champions in a World Cup tie at Murrayfield. South Africa won, van der Westhuizen scored a try. It was almost routine.

From memory, the last time I got to play against him was in 2001, when Scotland faced the Barbarians in a memorial match for 'Broon frae Troon', the late Gordon Brown. Guess what. Another try from van der Westhuizen, although that day probably belonged to another rugby great, sadly no longer here today: All Blacks legend Jonah Lomu, who scored four tries.

By then, Joost was already installed as one of the best number nines of all time. He was a big guy who had a real presence, but coupling that to his speed, especially off the mark, his fast, flat pass, dexterity and determination to win, made him a phenomenal player.

Whereas in Scotland we had wee, nippy, yappy, greetin'-faced scrum-halves – think about any of them in the last thirty years – Joost was a big unit who really fancied his chances against anyone. Just a brilliant player.

The next time we met, he was in a wheelchair. It was quite frightening, his deterioration.

I can't remember when or where I found out about his diagnosis – it would have been a few years before – but in 2013 Joost was across here with his brother and carer Pieter to raise awareness about MND and for his charity, the J9 Foundation. Euan MacDonald and his father Donald, who set up the Euan MacDonald Centre at Edinburgh University, were also at Murrayfield.

Joost's eyes were as piercing as ever, but although he was still in an upright chair then, he was struggling to speak and had to be fed and given drinks. It was terribly sad, especially given what an athlete he'd been, and very difficult not to get emotional. His eyes, though, told you he was still fighting.

Euan was there, in a bed, and I was trying to imagine how Joost must have felt, and what was he thinking, knowing that at some time in the future he would find himself in a similar position to Euan. It wasn't something you wanted to dwell on.

Joost did raise a smile with everyone when he had a wee drink. *Good on you*, I thought.

But remember, at this time, MND was simply something these guys had. My feelings towards them were entirely as unfortunate fellow men, dealt a rotten hand.

Jump forward to December 2016, and I find myself being given the same diagnosis. Unsurprisingly, Joost was one of the first people I thought about. And, within a few months, he was no longer here, passing away in the spring of 2017.

If my diagnosis was a hammer blow, Joost's passing was pretty devastating, absolutely shattering. In any sport, let alone rugby, during my lifetime he was the highest-profile MND sufferer. Would that mantle now fall to me?

It might, but that wasn't imminent, because except for a very few people, no one knew at that stage the news I'd been given. I had to play it with a straight bat.

Indeed, when Joost died in the February, I gave a couple of interviews, naturally talking about the times I'd played against him, and in particular that 1994 match, singing his deserved praises, but also knowing how close his story was to me now. That wasn't easy.

Neither was speaking to Joost's team. Joost had been quite ill, but I spoke to his brother, Pieter, and those at his J9 Foundation, just to find out what he'd been doing, what he had been taking, and whether there was any progress in treatment.

Unfortunately, they came back with a similar story to the

one I was already experiencing. Joost had tried everything, anything, and they'd gone from pillar to post to try and find something that might cause a positive reaction. It had been fruitless.

That was a shocking reality for me. Here was a man who had tried so much, had some great support within the rugby fraternity and in South Africa, had travelled around the world raising awareness, trying various therapies and drugs, and there was still nothing out there.

You kind of work that out for yourself, but that doesn't make it any easier to swallow.

You have a decision to make then: try the same course of action, or something different. Easier said than done when there doesn't appear to be anything different out there.

What had kept Joost alive, what had kept him going, had been his positivity. That was what his Foundation said and that was what I had to do – stay positive, stay focused on the future and what I wanted to be doing in the future.

Euan has had this for seven years. Joost was around for a long time after he'd been diagnosed – six years. But it's not having any accurate forecast, or timescale to work within, that makes it difficult. So, keeping yourself happy, staying positive, make that become your norm.

Has seeing Joost and Euan at Murrayfield that day helped me? In some ways, yes. It's as if you compartmentalise the various stages and how that will, eventually, impact on you. I've had my diagnosis; I am now living with it. Euan and Joost had to confront that in their own ways, because every case is different.

Those guys apart, and I greatly admire them, it was an

even bigger kick in the teeth when Stephen Hawking died after having battled Motor Neurone Disease for so long. I did go into my shell a wee bit with his passing, because it had finally caught up with someone who'd had it for so long.

I know old age could have played a part. But everything he achieved has spurred me on.

You do take stock, regardless of who it is, when you hear about another victim of MND. I'll give you an example, which really stung me, and again which makes you take a wee backward step momentarily. On the day of the Tartan Giraffe Ball in Kelso, I received an email from the brother-in-law of a thirty-eight-year-old who had been diagnosed in the September and succumbed in December. Three months. Left two kids, aged two and five. That takes the wind out your sails. It hit me quite hard, not that I knew the chap involved, but his circumstances seemed so familiar. Luckily, I was on my own when I read that email.

But it typifies the total randomness of MND. He lived fewer months than Stephen Hawking had survived decades. It is very difficult, impossible even, for you not to balance those stories and examples against your own circumstances. I thought about that chap's kids. I thought about my kids. It's great, working with some fantastically committed, dedicated people, raising money, raising the awareness of MND. But I don't think I would have had the fight, and the spirit, if it wasn't for the kids, Hamish, Angus and Ben. They are my constant inspiration to keep going, to keep fighting, because I want to see them leave school, pass driving tests, get their own house or car, find their own partners and relationships.

Take those highlights; take those individual and family landmarks. Now, put that into your own day-to-day life. How would you feel knowing you could miss all of that? And how would your children feel, not having you there to share those moments?

How would your wife, husband or partner cope?

Maybe you don't dwell on things for as long, or think it through to the nth degree. But you still run it through your head. That is just human nature.

And every time I hear about a death associated with MND, I have the same thoughts. It is not easy, and while people will see the smiles, the tartan suits, the one-liners and the interviews coming from me, behind that, on occasion, there is a lot going on.

But, we are where we are.

I'd have loved to have met Professor Hawking. He could have explained black holes; I could have explained line-out codes. One and the same thing really. Seriously, here was someone who'd battled MND for so long, over fifty years. But why was his death as upsetting as Joost, for instance?

Because, for me, you always look up to someone who has pushed the boundaries, gone beyond what was expected. Joost fought hard, but Stephen Hawking was given two years to live. That was back in the 1960s. Defying science. Quite a good goal, I think.

MND didn't get Stephen Hawking for a long time, and look at all the things he managed to do in that time. People from within his scientific community knew of him before MND took a grip. But for the rest of us, we only ever knew him as an MND sufferer. It didn't prevent him from becoming a celebrity or an author. Now, I am not going to write a couple of books on theoretical physics. Septic and sewage tanks, perhaps, although I don't know what the market might be like for those and this book has taken long enough to pen.

For me, Professor Hawking was the champion of MND, the exception who showed you could live with and survive MND, up to a point. Maybe his way of living wasn't the best. But he did live. And that has to be my goal, my ambition, and my source of positivity.

9

Coming Out

CONSULTANTS, DOCTORS, NURSES and carers knew, as did my family. However, sharing the word with the world that I'd been diagnosed with MND was something, if at all possible, that I wanted to handle my way.

Me and my family were still trying to come to terms with the news we'd been given at Christmas. We were still emotional, still tender, still living with the unknown. And me, I was still trying to get my head around the prospect of people suddenly changing their attitude towards me. I didn't want that. In fact, that would have been very difficult to take in those early days.

I was, genuinely, frightened that people would back off, stay away, become distant. I thought about it a lot.

Oh, I know you'll say that would never have happened. But then I never thought MND would happen. You begin to think, and rethink, every move you want to make or play out. That is particularly true around other people.

More than a year on from when I went public about my condition, I see it daily when I meet and greet folk. No one has ever shunned me or turned away. Everyone is polite, some more talkative than others, which is entirely as you would expect it. No two people are exactly the same, either emotionally or in how they handle a particular situation. But some put their hand on me, almost as if I'll break if they apply any pressure, while others just want to hug me, men and women. That kind of warmth and affection can be tear-jerking at times. And that's just from the men.

Going back to the early spring of 2017, I had my mind made up about how I was going to tackle things, and I knew two things – who I could trust, and who would still look upon me as Doddie, their pal, the big daftie. That, more than a number of other things, was important to me at the time. I needed that security. And, to be fair, it has never wavered or changed. I must be a good judge, or maybe I've just got good pals.

Actually, I knew three things, the third one being that the more people who knew, the more chance there was of it becoming public knowledge. Hence why I needed to get the first two things spot on.

I wanted people, especially the hundreds if not thousands I know, to know about me and my condition, but I wanted to be the one who told them.

There might have been a lorry-load of naivety on my part at the outset, thinking I could control that drip-feed of information. But by working with some fantastic indi-viduals, and maybe with a sprinkling of genius, trust and good luck along the way, we managed to keep the news under wraps until I was ready to tell the world. And there was very good reason for doing things in that manner.

MND is a dreadful thing, life-ending. But my life couldn't suddenly come to an abrupt halt because of some news I'd been given. I still had to work, make a living, and that meant doing all the things I'd been doing previously: farming, selling and installing septic tanks, broadcasting and after-dinner speaking.

If I had come out on day one and told everyone about my MND, how might those things have been affected? I wasn't going to take the chance. I still had to earn to live, for the future, even if it might not be my future.

For want of a better description, I was buying time, to show folk that nothing had changed, that I still could measure up and plan the installation of a sewage tank, that I could comment with some authority on the Melrose Sevens for the BBC (although some would say that would be a first), or that I could do a speaking engagement and entertain seven hundred people at Murrayfield (and many would say that would also have been a first!).

Yes, I could be accused of not being entirely honest with certain people. But was it their business to know my business at that time?

Nevertheless, there were people who I was going to have to tell, namely those close friends who me, Kathy and the boys would need going forward, to make some of my plans and ideas and dreams a reality. That wasn't easy. It was like telling family again, and again, and the emotion – after picking them off the floor, or helping them catch their breath – was just as raw every time.

One or two were slightly more, how can I put it, forthright in their acceptance of the situation. Gary Armstrong and Stewart Weir, who I've known as friends, beyond rugby and media, for well over twenty years, interspersed their dismay, shock, and even anger, with the odd expletive. One asked what the punchline was; the other, when told that I had MND, asked, 'Why the f*** would you want that?' Even in those circumstances, it was hard not to laugh.

If anything, their approach to the situation has got worse. People who don't do black humour should look away now. For instance, Gary said the road up to the farm would have to be repaired otherwise my mobility chair might disappear into one of the potholes. Stewart, meanwhile, said that while I might not be here, I couldn't really have visitors breaking the suspension on their cars when coming to pay their respects.

Now, not everyone will see the amusement I see in those comments. In such circumstances, some people may be a bit shocked.

When Stewart wrote a newspaper article the day after I'd gone public, he referred to me seeking a magic bullet, or a get out of jail card, or a Willy Wonka golden ticket that might just come to my rescue. For that, he got a letter, as he put it, from 'Mr Angry of Milngavie' who accused him of being 'flippant and unsympathetic' towards a poor man 'whose life could be cut short'.

To my mind, such an accusation is a mile off the mark. Stewart was telling it as he saw it, and he was bang on the money given the options available to me then and currently.

We all have to strike a serious note occasionally. But that should never be at the expense of doing the things I have loved and thrived on over the years: I love the banter, and it's what you get among friends, especially in rugby circles. I would never want that craic to change, and I don't see it happening anytime soon with that pair.

Maybe this is revenge for what I did to them. Because, when I started telling my 'inner circle' my news, I inadvertently omitted to tell them who else knew. I maybe hadn't considered that minor detail. I knew who knew. I just hadn't passed that info on. Silly me. If it ever happens again . . .

Which meant that not long after I'd informed Gary and Stewart, the pair of them went on a trip together, up to one of our favourite haunts, Loch Fyne Oysters, almost speaking in code there and back, trying to ascertain who knew what, if anything.

It wasn't until the next morning that Gary rang me to find out what Stewart knew. That must have been a strange car journey. In fact, 'strange' pretty much covers any time in a car with that pair.

Gary and Stewart knew early on, and so did Finlay Calder and John Jeffrey – again, friends and former colleagues with Scotland. Carl Hogg is someone I've known, some might say for too long. I didn't get the chance to tell him personally, so it needed to be done on the phone.

Four or five calls later, I lost count, but I still don't think I'd told him fully. It was excruciatingly emotional for both of us. The pair of us has been through a lot together, most of it self-inflicted in one shape or form. We go back a very long way, great pals whether it involved rugby or not. Now, attempting to tell him that it might come to an end, sooner than any of us wanted, was hard, very hard, almost impossible. But it needed to be done.

Hoggy's wife Jill (that'll be 'Jill with a J') is, again, someone I've known and liked for a long time, despite her coming from Hawick. Again, she was one of the first to be told and someone who I wanted on board when it came to taking my ideas for the future forward.

But that wasn't an easy time either. 'Tap dancing on eggshells' was how someone put it, and they weren't too far wide of the mark. Who do you tell, and when?

There were those who had to know, those who I wanted to know, and then a whole lot more who probably deserved to be told, but who, because of the complexity of the situation, just couldn't be informed at that time.

Thankfully, everyone understood my reasoning behind those decisions. I apologised several times to people for not telling them, or for how shocked they must have been when they heard the news. I was told time and again there was no need to say sorry. They understood and couldn't imagine what it has been like for me. It made me feel better, because as I said, there were folk close to me who really did deserve to know sooner. We'd just never had to deal with MND before.

But, while keeping my news under wraps, consideration had to be given to when I was going to go public, or, worse still, what if it went public before I was ready.

A few months after diagnosis, early in February 2017, suddenly, and completely out of the blue, I received a text from my ex-Falcons colleague Marius Hurter.

He pinged me a message on WhatsApp, which, to be honest, I didn't even know I was connected to, just to ask if this was still my number and what was I up to.

I replied, saying it was my number, and that it was all good with me and the family, and passed on my sympathies to him that his former World Cup-winning teammate Joost van der Westhuizen had sadly passed away after his battle with Motor Neurone Disease.

What came back completely threw me. 'Hearing rumours about your health, thinking about you and the family. Hope all is good.'

I hadn't seen this one coming. Had it been some tittle-tattle around the Borders, in Selkirk, or Lauder, or even in rugby circles, perhaps I could have understood it. But that the word was out, halfway around the world?

I sat on it for a day, then mentioned it during a chat with Stewart, who was the one I'd discussed it with – how we'd eventually make the announcement. There was then a plan put in place whereby we could go public with a statement, that 'due to speculation' here was me confirming my condition. That was Plan B.

Plan A, on the other hand, was slightly more convoluted. However, 'slightly more convoluted' may well be a phrase that those involved with it all will read now and probably spit their wine over the dog, or have someone's eye out with the remnants of a Ferrero Rocher. The goalposts shifted a few times along the way, with me doing the shifting.

There was never going to be an easy or a good time to break this story. And it was a story on a number of fronts. Firstly from the public interest perspective, but also because of how I wanted to make the news known, and why.

I was never going to hide it – I've never hidden in my life, and that has nothing to do with my stature. I would front up MND and, if possible, would be a front for MND sufferers, many of whom, literally, needed a voice.

After telling my immediate family and friends, workwise, I was right in to one of my busiest periods, namely the Six Nations, where I did quite a lot of hosting, hospitality work and after-dinner speaking engagements, many of them through the Murrayfield Experience during Scotland's home Test matches.

In short, I wanted that out of the way first. It wouldn't have been impossible to do my bit, entertaining five and six hundred people at Murrayfield, had the word got out, but it would have been difficult. And not just for me.

I had to think about those at the Scottish Rugby Union who had employed me, and the guests who were turning up to have a right good day out. Would my news subdue them, make it less enjoyable and, again, what would the reaction be towards me?

No, we were doing it after. Plan B was there, as back-up. But Plan A was, initially, to reveal all after the Six Nations had run its course. And although that text from Marius didn't quite cause a panic, it did make us aware that the longer we left it, the more chance there was of us having less control over events.

Stewart simply asked if Marius was sound. That took all of two seconds to answer. He and I had become great friends, and we still are. When he arrived over from South Africa, I was the guarantor for his first car. His way of thanking me was to give me some very exclusive South African wine, and some instructions, which I didn't pay much attention to.

Of course, me being me, I brought out this wine for a Christmas lunch I was having with Kathy and her family, boasting that this was one of the most sought-after wines from the Cape, opened it up and nearly poisoned everyone. It was disgusting.

Needless to say, Marius's 'instruction' that had completely gone over my head – not being a wine lover – was to let it sit for three or four years. I listen now when I get handed any wines or spirits!

As a person, a teammate and a friend, I'd put a lot of trust in Marius back then, not to drop me at line-outs, to keep up payments on his new wheels, and not to bugger off and leave me with a car. But that was nothing to the trust that I was placing on his broad, sculpted shoulders this time around.

There was part of me wanted to know what he knew and how he knew it. But that could have made things more open and therefore awkward. Eventually I replied and told him yes, we had a wee issue, but that I was keeping it quiet for now. I knew Marius wouldn't break ranks.

Plan A was back to the fore, and we would see out the Six Nations and then break the news. That was the plan. But you know how the best laid plans sometimes don't quite work out?

Hindsight, as I have found out a few times over recent months, is always 20/20. It was only once the Six Nations had reached its conclusion that I took stock of where we were, namely in the middle of March. How did that happen?

Time flies when you are enjoying yourself, as they say,

and the Six Nations, meeting and seeing old pals and team-mates, is always a hoot. Brilliant days, even better banter, with nice beer and whisky thrown in.

But suddenly the best part of three months had gone, and I was still sitting on my revelation. So far, so good. Except it wasn't good in the slightest.

I was still walking, talking, living and breathing. But what I was now very aware of was that we were just weeks away from Hamish sitting his final exams at school. There had been enough for him to contend with and to overcome up until this point in time, but the whole brouhaha, the whole circus that may arise around me after making it known I had MND, I felt might be a wrecking ball to his chances of leaving school with the results and grades he would have wanted, and that he deserved considering everything that he was having to contend with in his life.

I didn't want my world imploding into his.

It wasn't an easy decision to make, like so many over the past couple of years, but thinking of Hamish more than anything, I decided to delay coming out a bit longer, until his exams were done.

To be fair, those I talked it over with the most – namely Jill and Stewart – fully understood the circumstances. 'What are you like?' laughed Jill, seeing the funny side of plans unravelling and being hastily redrawn.

We weighed up the options, all of them, and they were fine with my reasoning, probably seeing it as parents them-selves. Not parents together, obviously, I think.

Secretly, in terms of how well they know the media industry, they might have been having kittens. But they kept it well hidden, although there was probably a very large collective sigh of relief once we did break the news.

I mentioned earlier about worlds imploding, but, as if by chance, all of our collective planets appeared to align, although one or two had to be given a wee nudge so to speak.

It had always been my dream, aim, ambition, whatever way you want to describe it, that I would take Kathy and the boys to South Africa in 2021 for the Lions tour there. I'd loved the country so much when I'd gone there with Scotland in 1995 for the World Cup and – briefly (through no fault of my own) – in 1997 with the Lions, and I wanted them to see and experience what a great country it is.

That was the plan, but so much of what we had looked to in the future was suddenly being fast-forwarded because we weren't sure just how long I had. What were the chances of me being diagnosed with MND coinciding with the British & Irish Lions touring New Zealand in 2017? Probably quite remote, to be completely honest. And being totally honest again, quite remote were my chances of getting to share a Lions tour with the wife and family.

We had started to make tentative enquiries into the practicalities and the costs involved in taking on a trip to New Zealand. It was not going to be easy, or cheap. Prices were at a premium now, simply because of all the tour packages that had been purchased. Lions trips are big business, for those involved and for the fans. But this one seemed bigger than most.

Then, someone stepped forward and offered to pay for our flights, business class no less, to New Zealand. It was

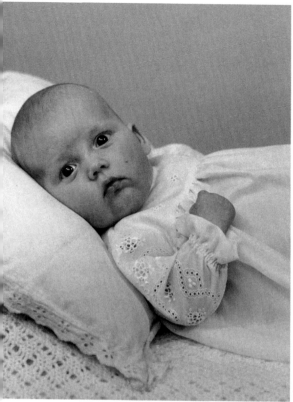

What a braw laddie, born on the 4th of July.

The Cowboy and Bull – great name for a pub.

The huntsman – with hound.

Me, Kirsty and Thomas in Blackpool.

Silverware – a bit young to be filling it though.

The magnificent Arpal Glider –
and my long legs!

Me feeding the lovely Betty.

Our big day – I had to make an effort.

This was why I kept
her number.

I think this is a fancy dress party.

Our honeymoon on Mauritius.

Hamish with, or rather in,
the Tetley Bitter Cup.

A back row in the making –
Hamish, Angus and Ben.

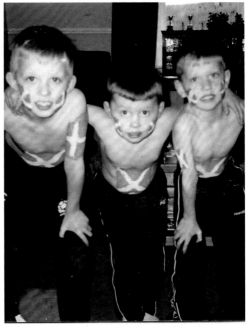

Me, Hamish and a young Angus.

Back row boys – too good looking
to be in the front row.

Curry night with
Tony Underwood.

With niece Alex and nephew Jack,
and Jonny Wilkinson.

Trying to convince people
I'm Scottish.

Lock out – Ian Jones, John Eales, Gary Whetton,
Chris Gray and me.

Me, David Sole, Tony Stanger, Craig Redpath,
Dougie Wyllie and Sean Lineen and a farewell
Haka in New Zealand.

2002: Gary, me, George, Pat and
Inga say farewell to the Falcons.
2018: Us again, but with Rob
Andrew replacing Inga. Well,
they have the same size wallets!

An early nursery picture of me and Toony.

The young, lean and mean look.

Sevens victory – winning my 'home' Melrose Sevens with the Co-Optimists.

Captain fantastic: lifting the Tetley Bitter Cup.

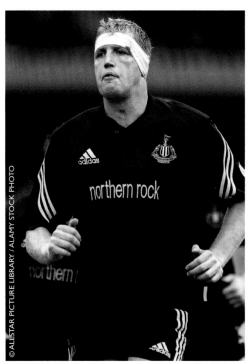

The older, filled out and battered look.

Celebrating winning the
English Premiership title.

an act of amazing generosity, one of many around that time and since.

Now, it has never been in my nature to accept such gifts. A beer, or two, yes, but that can be reciprocated. But people putting their hand in their pocket to help me. Why?

I've had the reasoning explained to me – because of who you are, what you've done, your predicament. Do I deserve that?

The answer, not mine but one I've been given a few times now, is yes. Why? Because people, taking a step back and being quite dispassionate about what has happened, tell me I'd have done the same thing myself. They might be right.

It was very hard though, particularly at the outset of this journey, for me to get my head around why people would want to be so kind to me and my family. It still makes me uncomfortable. However, I have had to accept it and live with it. Not easy, and still quite humbling, although nobody sets out with that intention. That's just me being me.

But what is it they say about old dogs and new tricks? I quickly realised my energy would be better served driving me forward, for longer, than getting drawn into arguments, albeit very friendly and at times funny arguments, with people who would not take no for an answer.

The person in question, who donated our flights to New Zealand, I would say is as immovable as me when it comes to standing his ground. He would not listen to my protests, he would not enter into any conversation about it, except to say it was what he wanted to do, and what he wanted me to do was accept the gift and head off to New Zealand.

I thanked him, but only to his face. He didn't want it

made public, something that others too have stipulated when supporting me and my family. I will be eternally grateful for their generosity at that time, and to those who have been equally forthcoming in their support of me, and subsequently the Trust and Foundation.

But, back to the timetable, and how we were going to get the word out on me and MND.

Hamish's exams were completed, May into June. And June, coincidentally, was when MND Awareness Week was scheduled. Could we extend the self-imposed embargo for another two or three weeks?

By now there were wee rumblings, and I was aware of various things that had been said. I wasn't upset by that. The real upset would have been in dealing with it coming out through a third party. I had already taken stock though; I knew that when it had come to staying quiet on my news that actually, in the grand scheme of things, I had led quite a charmed existence.

What we were aware of, however, was that those who suspected something was wrong had said nothing, almost keeping their thoughts to themselves. And those who were sure they knew something was afoot, adopted almost the rugby equivalent of 'omertà', akin to a vow of silence.

Therefore, having got this far into the year, without anyone saying a word, we felt quite confident we'd get away with it for those few additional days and weeks, and so it proved.

By the time Motor Neurone Awareness Day came around, we were ready to go. I was still apprehensive about the response we might receive, but the relief of being honest with the world far outweighed any negativity or hassle that may have arisen.

I needn't have worried, because it all went so seamlessly, most of that down to how well coordinated a plan Stewart and Jill had put in place. Rather than having to deal with any intrusion back home, they had worked out that I would be headed to the rugby-friendly environment of New Zealand, where rugby players receive more of a reverential reception. Remember, too, that their islands and cities would be full of British & Irish Lions fans as well, who would be nothing less than one hundred per cent supportive towards me. And it was exactly like that.

We had already left for New Zealand and, after our stopover in Dubai and at a height of 39,000 feet over the Indian Ocean, the button was pressed and a media statement was released. The world knew.

I say the world, with probably one exception. Me.

Having been given a list of what to do, and more importantly what I shouldn't do, the main one being not to answer my phone, texts or emails, I decided that the safest and easiest way to avoid all contact with the outside world was to remove the SIM card from my phone, stand on it, and scrunch it into the tarmac. I know, how very Luddite – and what a stupid thing to do. I realised that after a few days out there.

But for a technophobe like myself, who still marvels at the difference between diesel and petrol (and who really wanted to avoid roaming charges) it seemed a very sound response. What did I say about hindsight?

Correct, I wouldn't have done it if I'd known the hassle it

would cause. As a result of my hammer to crack a walnut approach, my family became my messengers, both delivering and receiving correspondence from various people, and following social media along with those back at home, who were fielding the rest of the countless enquiries and requests.

I might have become a popular person around that time. But I don't think my family and friends saw it that way.

Still, I could sit back, chill and enjoy the rugby and the beer and try not to think too much about ever being able to do – or getting to do – this again. A lot easier said than done.

10

Lions 1997

THE BRITISH & IRISH LIONS TOUR to New Zealand in the summer of 2017 took on an added significance, entirely because of the news delivered to me just a few months before. It also brought sharply into focus again my own experiences as a tourist twenty years prior.

I'd had a good couple of years playing with Scotland, only missing out in both 1995 and 1996 on a Grand Slam when England proved to be slightly better than us, thus depriving me of legendary status like the teams of '84 and '90, and therefore a couple of extra chapters for this book.

At club level, with Newcastle winning promotion, 1996/97 was a great year for me and although a title would have been nice, it was job done in terms of being up among the big boys.

However, the actual reality was that we were the big boys, albeit from the lower leagues, as were the guys from Richmond. Apart from us Newcastle boys, the lads from Richmond – Allan Bateman and Scott Quinnell – were, like us, going with the Lions, having been second division players in England that season. Some would say I was never anything better than second division, and who could argue. But on that occasion, the Lions selectors got their choice spot on.

But our inclusion, and that of the former Rugby League boys, only typified the upheaval and revolution that was going on within the English professional game around that time.

The professional era heralded a change in rugby. Much of it was down to club ownership, hard cash, and the players you could recruit. It took a few years for things to shake out and for there to be some stability within the league structure in England. That meant that what you had leading up to that Lions tour were several contenders and candidates who were playing outside of the top grade.

It also meant that for the first time, in this new 'open' era, management and selectors had a free hand to pick who they wanted. Ian McGeechan was, as usual, ahead of the curve on that one. Personally, I don't think that went down well with certain parties within the establishment, Union men to the core, who had been finding it difficult to accommodate individuals and changes in the game, never mind having to contend with an institution like the Lions welcoming some of these 'Northern sorts' who'd had the audacity to play for filthy lucre before we had. We are, of course, talking about the ex-League boys here who, to a man, never slacked or gave anything less than their max.

I for one didn't have an issue, not when Rob Andrew had gone on a spending spree to turn the Falcons into the best team in English – if not European – rugby, with a side full of guys from the thirteen-a-side code. The involvement of the League guys lifted the level of professionalism in the Lions squad to new heights. I knew how the League guys played and conditioned themselves. They were, in effect, setting the benchmark for everyone in the Lions squad to match.

Four years before, I had been on some reserve or replacement list for the Lions when they went to New Zealand, without getting a call. That gets you thinking about what might have been, and what might be in the future with equal measures of good form and fortune. Playing for a big club was great, for your country even better. But the Lions, to be able to say that you had been one, was something to be proud of – that you were the best, in your position, among the four home nations. I'm not being boastful or bragging, but I bet there isn't a player selected for the Lions who hasn't puffed his chest out, or drawn himself up to his full height, or smiled quietly to himself, when that letter was delivered. It is just such a great feeling.

Not only was it my passport to go on that tour, but it was my membership to a very special – you might say totally unique – club, which will never leave you. And they have never left me. What they did last summer in New Zealand was evidence of that.

Back in 1997, the indications were that I was well placed to make that trip. Various journalists, some of them better connected than others, had been speculating about who would be selected. I'd appeared in a few polls, and then not on another. But what did they know about rugby?

There had been a few nudges, winks and hints dropped

long before the official party was named, and the letter came through with me in there as one of only five Scots in the initial squad, along with my Newcastle teammate Alan Tait, Gregor 'Toony' Townsend, Tom 'Tammy Troot' Smith and the good doctor, Rob Wainwright. I was also in the company of some of my Falcons pals, John 'Bentos' Bentley, Taity, another one of the Rugby League heathens, Tim Stimpson and Tony Underpants (sorry, Underwood).

But while I had a foot in a couple of camps, it was drilled into us from the off that there would be no cliques, no wee groups, no 'us and them'. We were there representing the Lions. It might have been as representatives of four nations, but we were now as one, and would have to breathe deep, work together and believe that we were the best if we were going to come away from a Test series against the reigning world champions with any level of credibility or success.

We gathered at our Surrey base, the Oatland Park Hotel in Bagshot, for a week of bonding sessions as well as intensive training – physical, mental and media. We were treated so well, to the best of everything. It was the first hotel I'd been in where you could watch TV and be on the phone at the same time while sitting on the toilet. Certain things you forget in your career, that isn't one of them.

It was during this week of preparation that Jim Telfer applied his mechanics and method, perhaps even his madness, to the forwards preparation.

Now, for me and the other Scots boys, this was just normal, Jim being Jim. He used a carrot and stick approach, without the carrot, but there was a real stick. He used his stick to demonstrate angles with body position, in the scrum, in the drive, in the tackle. It also came in handy when putting his point across if he felt he was being ignored.

He was the boss and he was always right. Even when you got it right, with Jim's psychology, you were actually only less wrong than you'd been previously. It was a punishing, gruelling, jaw-dropping, eye-opening week for the Irish, Welsh and English boys.

One of my fellow Celts replied, 'You are f***ing kidding me,' when I told him that by day, back home, Jim was a highly respected headmaster.

'Is he always like this?' asked one of the English members, who admitted they'd never seen or heard anything like it before.

'No, it's early days yet, quiet for him. You'll see the real him once we get to South Africa,' I promised. And we did. He had one scrummaging session that lasted an hour. I had never seen a bunch of players look so exhausted, physically. Their eyes told you that they had given everything.

What wasn't given was a backward step or any quarter. The live scrummaging sessions were a bit tasty on occasions. Even in training, people were putting a marker down.

Jim was the peacemaker. Then he shouted at them, swore at them, screamed at them that he wanted more of the same.

Wainwright, Smith and me, most of the time, weren't too upset, having developed an immune system to Jim's torture treatment. But it didn't matter about nationality, how many caps, tours or Grand Slams you had, you were fair game. He asked questions of every single forward, and made you think about everything you were doing.

What was not in question, and was never doubted then

or since, was that the success of the Lions on that tour owed much to the relationship between McGeechan, the diplomat and slightly quieter, more measured assassin, and Telfer, the occasionally less diplomatic general.

In some ways, they were conformists, as in making sure the simple things were done correctly. Five yards from the opposition line, be it a scrum or a line-out, you knew what the stock move and call would be. The try Wainwright scored against Border was a classic example: take, drop, roll, score. We'd have practised that fifty times.

But both of them had an eye for individualism, that off-the-cuff play someone would pull out the bag, making something out of nothing. It may have been down to the players, yes. Neither Ian nor Jim did anything to quell or suppress the talent people possessed.

And that entire tour was full of moments of genius. Matt Dawson throwing the dummy overhead that sent the entire Cape the wrong way. Jeremy Guscott deciding 'now is a good time to try a drop goal' in that Second Test. Bentley becoming a Ferrari whenever he was given ten yards to run into. And who knew what Toony would do any of the time, even Toony himself.

In the case of Telfer, he instilled absolute and complete belief, discipline and respect within those forwards. He knew where you had to be, and he also decided very early on with one or two whether they could or couldn't make it. But he was always going to give you every opportunity to prove yourself. Reputation was one thing. But it was what they saw in you on tour that decided whether you had what it took at Test level.

The coaching style of today is that you have to take away a positive thought from every session, that you're the best, that the man next to you is the best. Jim was slightly different. As we left a training session our main hope was that we might be less shite tomorrow.

'Away hame and don't come back if you are going to do the same tomorrow.'

I often wondered what the fallout would have been had we taken him at his word, except none of us were brave enough to find out.

Did his style work for me? Absolutely, even if he told me and others at various times that we'd let ourselves down, our teammates down, our school, families, friends, the country.

However, personally, I don't think it is coincidental that some of the greatest players in the history of Melrose and Scotland, even the Lions, have been crafted by the Telfer ways.

Even now, when a bunch of us get together from Melrose, Scotland or the Lions, we'll have a laugh and a joke at Jim's expense. He has mellowed and can look back and laugh at himself. But, to a man, deep down, we all know that a good part of anything we achieved came down to what he drilled into us.

Ian McGeechan was different in his ability to pick up on smaller details. For instance, if one of the backs ran in a certain way, he knew if he was going to pass, because his hands were in a certain position, compared to whether he was going to make a line break or run. If Geech could pick that out, so too could the South Africans. So, he made people think about what they were going to do, almost reprogrammed you to make it less obvious what was coming.

They were meticulous, incredibly switched on. That was when you knew just how much thinking had gone on in the four years between New Zealand and South Africa, into who was there, how they'd be used, and exactly the method that would be employed as to how the Lions were going to beat the reigning world champions. They were passionate rugby men, passionate about bringing success to the Lions, as was Fran Cotton.

However, before anyone thinks it was oval-shaped purgatory, there was light relief in abundance down at Bagshot, in the form of the team-bonding games, as well as the media training we received, which is where my now famous 'mistaken identity' line came from. I still think it showed my razor-sharp reactions at their best. For those who aren't familiar with the moment, a scenario was posed of me having been seen in a nightclub by South African journalists, and I was asked to respond, hence the 'mistaken identity' quip.

When asked who it might have been, I replied, 'My father is on tour.' And the rest is a piece of viral social media, made possible by a very bold decision agreed upon by the Lions hierarchy.

Introducing the TV cameras and making the official tour video, *Living With Lions*, could have gone horribly wrong. It transpired that it was one of the best sporting documentaries ever. Winning the series helped. Had we lost, that video camera would have been one of the grounds for failure, make no mistake. But for me, it took the Lions to a new level.

People at home saw first-hand what it meant to everyone involved, the calculated approach of Geech, the unbridled winning mentality of Telfer and, above all else, what it meant to pull on that Lions jersey. Other tours may have been less successful, but no one would ever think touring was a sightseeing jolly from then on.

With regard to the video, the editing was a masterpiece of cinematography. Some of the footage shot once we were in South Africa, particularly by Bentos, was borderline between comedy classic and criminal offence. His running commentary and insightful questioning – 'What are you doing, Doddie?' – when you were sitting on the toilet, really was award-winning.

Bentos had a number of rivals, like 'Take 17' Wainwright, who opened every interview with the same questions: 'Is it on? Can you see a red light?' Imagine if he was an airline pilot or the captain of a ship. 'Can you see a red light?' Thankfully, he's only a doctor.

At our Surrey HQ, much time – and no doubt money – was spent on those bonding sessions. The games played were about getting everyone thinking the same, cooperating as a group – as one, not as individuals – and working together for a common aim or goal, or to solve a problem, which usually involved building something, moving something or somebody, without using your hands, and gallons of water.

It was good fun, but most of us had worked out it was just a way of making the England players feel wanted and giving the Irish, Welsh and Scots a reason for talking to them.

For me, the real bonding session, and when we became brothers in arms, was when Fran Cotton, a real stalwart of all things Lions, clapped his hands on the Friday afternoon and said, 'Well done, right, pub.' For me, that was when we became as one, a team.

Once we got out there, the team ethos was again evident. The social and players committee struck a wonderful balance between work and play. I'd best describe it as being kept on a very long chain. We trusted each other and, for me, not breaking or damaging that bond meant much more than any possible fine or punishment that the management could have brought to bear.

I also got the impression that with Fran, Ian and Jim, they'd all been young themselves once upon a time, and weren't really frightened to let us out of their sight. I don't think we were nannied in the same way others have been since.

In terms of who you roomed with, that was another area where it was never 'them and us'. It was mixed up, no one sharing with a countryman where possible, or a back. They just think too much.

Living on a farm, I was well used to seeing what animals would be happy to sleep in, but even livestock had standards above some teammates.

Take Richard Hill, for instance. He was a fantastic guy, one I really got to know and like on that trip and one who has remained a friend ever since. But, in terms of bedroom manners, he was abysmal. You were never quite sure if your room had been ransacked, stormed by an elite squad of South African special forces or if a tornado had blown through the room. Boots and trainers lying everywhere, socks on radiators (that most of the time weren't even switched on), pants on lampshades, towels dumped. And then he asked had I seen his wallet or pen.

Martin Johnson was the captain and another I shared with. Jonno was very quiet, or so I thought then. Looking back, it was a wee bit difficult to be sharing with someone who ultimately you were trying to stick on the bench.

You pick a Lions captain based on who you think will be irreplaceable or immovable from your first choice Test side. Jonno fitted that billing. He also looked down on the South African captain Gary Teichmann. That was the psychology at play.

However, with Jonners nailed on, that meant me, Shawsy (Simon Shaw) and Buzz Lightyear (Jeremy Davidson) were, in principle, all playing for the other berth at lock from the off. It didn't trouble me. I was up for the challenge and, if someone was better, good luck to them. It wasn't as if the team would be selected out of a hat. Someone being considered better than you, that happens when opinions and preferences come into play. But I was determined to give myself every chance of being in the Lions Test side come Cape Town a month or so after we'd first hit South African soil.

With Martin sitting out the first game – he'd just come off a domestic season where he played forty-plus games – Jason Leonard captained the team and I started, paired with Simon Shaw, as we beat an Eastern Province select 39–11 and I scored with a sixty-metre, jinking, side-stepping run, rounded off with a dramatic dive over from distance. Well, that's how I see it in my mind.

Jason was an absolute rock on the corner of the scrum. It

was like being behind Iain Milne in my early Scotland days. They did all the work in the scrum and you could have a wee breather. Lovely. But he was one of the other captains on that trip, as was Keith Wood, who was just phenomenal as a teammate and a super tourer. As a person, for me, Woody probably epitomised the whole Lions ethos more than anyone. To me, he was a confidante, an inspiration, and just a man who got the importance of what went on, both on and off the field. He liked a beer, liked a laugh, and could indulge in a bit of nonsense. I would say he could let his hair down, if he had any. But there was a time for work and a time to play, and he was a brilliant judge of mood, knowing when players and the team needed lifting, or when they needed to be brought down to earth, or just left alone. A good stag party organiser, as well.

I'd say 'Uncle Fester' would be a brilliant Lions tour manager in the future, if he ever wanted to be considered for that role.

Rob Wainwright, again someone I knew through Scotland, and Tom Smith likewise, became really good friends during that trip, and we will to this day share a dram or several, or a red wine, in each other's company.

These friendships and associations developed, just as the team did. Second game up would be against Border, and again I was named in the starting XV with Jeremy packing down alongside me.

It was a wet, muddy, windy day, the game a dour, unspectacular grind which we won eventually 18–14, with captain-for-the-day Wainwright scoring the try off my line-out catch to nose in front late on. That match provided the first heart-stopping moment on the trip, when Scott Gibbs was stretchered off with an ankle injury. You don't like seeing anyone being crocked, but it felt particularly significant that early in proceedings, and when it was our own squad carrying off one of our own. As it transpired, it wasn't too bad.

From East London, it was upward and onward with a flight to Cape Town. I think that was when I started to feel like the tour was cranking up. There were demands on our time outside the rugby and training, like the public appearances, and the private ones, such as an official reception at the British High Commission.

That was an opportunity to meet people who lived and worked in South Africa, each of them very supportive of us being there and what we were trying to achieve.

The fantastic Newlands hosted the meeting with Western Province, and I got to spectate as Jonno entered the fold. Another win, then a flight up country to face Mpumalanga, and I was back in the team, paired with Jeremy again. We also had another captain, Tim Rodber. Maybe I was wrong about the tour captain being guaranteed his place. A few hours later, it mattered little.

Things were going to plan, inasmuch as we were winning, and winning well. And I don't really remember much about the game, other than when I was trying to get my boot on the ball at a ruck, I got this sting in my knee. Two things crossed my mind. One was, *That didn't feel good.* The other was, *Where did that come from?*

I reeled away – hopped away actually – unable and unwilling to put any weight on my leg, as I couldn't really feel where I was putting it down. I still wasn't fully aware of what had happened, but I knew from the way some of the players on the pitch and the medics were looking at me that it couldn't have been good. I was off, leg up, iced up.

One thing that evolved very quickly in the professional era was the level of medical supervision that players commanded. I suppose if you were paying large fees and salaries for talent, and with a duty of care to your employees, you would want to be covered on that front.

For some time we had with Scotland been cared for by Dr James Robson, a man who I and the rest of the Scots boys trusted implicitly, the best in the business. Ironic then, that he would be the one who delivered the news that the medial ligament in my left knee had gone. No need to ask if he was kidding. He didn't kid much.

No, it was serious, no chance of resting to repair the damage. It was job over, all caught on camera, as it happened. Not stunted, no additional takes, just totally raw. It would need fixed and my tour was at an end.

I thought I held it together quite well, on the outside. Inside, my stomach churned and I really wanted to scream, not in agony, not at the news – injuries will always be part and parcel of rugby. But at the way I'd been booted out the tour.

That night, I was driven to Johannesburg for a scan. It was an unexpected guided tour of the parts that weren't on any tourist itinerary. It was scary.

There were people running after our car – our Range Rover stood out a bit – and we had to stop to ask for directions. We were quickly surrounded. I didn't know what was going on or what their intentions might be. What I did know was that, sat in a full leg brace, this wasn't really a situation or a place I wanted to be in.

Anyway, we found the hospital, had the scan, and confirmed the worst. Tour over.

Jim Telfer said nothing good ever came out of Mpumalanga, and I'd have to agree. I went back with Scotland in 1999 and yanked my knee again.

But on a Lions tour, you are exposed, almost, to these teams and players who are there to knock you down, and really don't care about the methods used to knock you down. That was and is dangerous and I could never see why touring players should be made to face that risk.

There are sanctions, yes. But while a six-month ban for an international may severely jeopardise his prospects and even career, a 26-week suspension for a part-timer or amateur probably means he can concentrate on working his farm. Not that Marius Bosman even got a suspension. He was fined £1,500 for ending my tour with an attack with which he could also have finished my career.

It was the same four years later in Australia when Duncan McRae battered Ronan O'Gara. Eight stitches equated to a seven-week suspension.

I get the fact that tours need to be of a certain length, in terms of the matches played, and that games have to be taken on as part of the preparations for the Test side. But these games need to be against players of a comparable standard, both in terms of ability and professionalism.

As I found out, that game was a ready-made opportunity for those sorts who would inflict hurt and damage on opposition players as the only way they knew of getting the better of them, simply because their lack of ability didn't allow for a fair contest.

For me, Marius Bosman was a classic example of that. He must have been thinking about how he could impact on the game, what he could do when being completely outplayed. Maybe being unable to make a meaningful contribution was causing intense frustration. I don't have to watch video re-runs of him stamping on my knee with such a force that my entire leg buckles. I felt it at the time.

I'm not one to look back and say I wonder what would have happened had I stayed on that tour. The biggest sadness for me was that I was leaving behind a great bunch of boys, on a trip where I had loved every minute of the experience. Staying and playing, maybe making a Test team, would have been fantastic. And then I could have had a disaster, a loss of form or, worst of all, been put back to number 8.

However, just staying on the tour would have been sufficient for me, staying with my pals as we zigzagged across the Cape, seeing the new places and faces, but Bosman denied me that through his malice and thuggery.

The unfortunate thing is his name – borrowed and bestowed upon the hedgehog boot-cleaner we had outside the back door of our house (eventually killed off by a combination of kicks and horse muck) – will still be brought up every time the Lions visit South Africa (as McRae's was in the most recent Lions tour of Australia), in effect celebrating his calculated and clinical stamp on my knee. His notoriety lives on, when really he deserves to be forgotten.

Thankfully my part with the British & Irish Lions wasn't

forgotten. I flew home – passing Mum and Dad who were coming in the opposite direction to see me – but was back by the end of the tour as a supporter, still wearing the official blazer. They weren't going to get rid of Lion number 670 that easily!

That bond still applies now. The British & Irish Lions have been fantastic in their support of me and my campaign, and receiving my Lions cap in the summer of 2018 – to celebrate the 130th anniversary of the Lions – was just such a fantastic honour, as it was for everyone recognised in that way.

It was brilliant seeing and sharing the delight of those I'd toured with in 1997, and even better witnessing those players who had toured more than half a century ago, but who only this year received what many might see as the greatest international honour, a cap from the British & Irish Lions.

In the one hundred and thirty years of the Lions just over eight hundred players have been selected to play for them. When you work this out, it means that at any one club there may only be a single player, or at best a handful of players, who have ever been selected for the Lions and, even then, some could be decades apart.

To be the best from these four nations, and for your peak to coincide with a cycle which only comes around every four years, makes being a Lion a unique honour and it is therefore a very special accolade you hold, a very special place in rugby history, and perhaps best of all, a very special place in the affections of rugby fans from these isles.

For me, in a playing sense, my Lions career lasted just

three games. However, I doubt that if I had appeared in another four or five games on that trip, or even another tour, that I'd be considered any more of a Lion. That's not the way it works.

Once you pull on that red jersey, with that badge on the front, your status is sealed for life. And off the back of that one tour, twenty years ago, I have received countless invites for speaking engagements and appearances, all because in British and Irish rugby circles, as well as those countries the Lions have visited, you are seen as being the best of the best.

And last year, thankfully, this former player got the chance to be one of those countless and dedicated supporters. If going in 1997 to South Africa was special, seeing the British & Irish Lions in New Zealand in 2017 was, through very different circumstances, every bit as memorable.

11

Welcome to New Zealand

BY THE TIME WE TOUCHED DOWN in New Zealand, the rugby fraternity on both sides of the planet were aware of our circumstances. How could I best describe the response we received? I'd call it a slow burner. People, whether we knew them or not, were obviously happy to give us time and space. Only then did some broach the subject, but a great many, while maybe wanting to say something, kept their thoughts to themselves.

I was fine with that. This was something of a learning curve for all concerned.

We picked up our campervan – a six-berth, although it was still cosy when I stretched out – and off we went.

One of the first people I bumped into was Scott 'there is only one Welsh legend in my family and it isn't me' Quinnell. I've known Scotty for a very long time, as a rival, as a fellow tourist, as a pundit and, of course, from various hospitality functions. That was, how can I put it, a bit raw, emotionally.

Nevertheless, there was an amusing side to it. Namely that Scott was out there for Sky Sports, slumming it in a campervan having lost the last of his 'League Of Their Own' challenges against Will Greenwood, another who I've got to know as one of the nicest former adversaries in rugby. While Quinnell was stuck in a van, going from place to place, having to hang out his own washing, Greenwood had his laundry done for him and was lording it in a Range Rover.

Those early days in New Zealand, after we'd touched down, were as hard as I've had to contend with, emotionally. Prior to leaving the UK, only a select few knew of my condition.

Now, you were never sure who knew, how they were going to approach you, or what they were going to say when they did.

Even the friendliest of approaches could stop you in your tracks.

What was a real tear-jerker, for me, was ahead of one of the games, when we were all sitting there in our red outfits, Lions supporters everywhere, and a chap came up to me and asked if these were my kids. I replied yes.

'Oh, lucky boys. I wish my dad had taken me on a trip like this to watch the Lions. You'll have memories forever.'

It was a nothing comment, the sort of thing I'd have said to others myself in the past. I take it he didn't know the real reason why we were all there. But I never explained to this chap the circumstances behind why, as a family, we were out in New Zealand. It was just too difficult and possibly embarrassing to him, and I wouldn't want that. A smile and nod became almost a stock answer.

But I wasn't thinking about just me. What was going on in the heads of the boys when they heard this? It could hardly be considered people prying into your life, or your emotions. Was general chit-chat going to be such a minefield of emotions? I knew I'd have much to contend with once my battle with MND became public knowledge. But having to second-guess how the boys and wife were feeling, that was tougher than I had bargained for. Again, I was learning, just about, to cope. But when it came to wondering what Kathy, Hamish, Angus and Ben were thinking or feeling, that really churned you inside. All you could do was ask if they were okay. They'd say yes, but you could tell with their eyes, or if they took a deep breath, how much it had affected them. I think once we got over those initial few days, it became a bit easier to roll with any accidental body-blows that were thrown.

★

Our journey had been wonderful, with no shortage of additional highlights thrown in along the way. We drove down the wine route on the South Island, visited the Hobbits (like a day trip to Kelso), and then went to Rotorua and had a go on the luge. I remember Gavin Hastings ripping the backside out of a new pair of jeans on it years ago. But my brother Thomas had no fear: 'What could go wrong?'

Quite a lot given he was attacked by his nephews Hamish and Jack, who ran him off the track and turned him upside down. Thankfully he didn't rip his denims. But he did scratch his Rolex.

We were helicoptered onto the top of a glacier, out of Queenstown on to the South Island, and then I went bungee jumping, twenty-five years after I'd first tried it. I'd forgotten what it felt like. There were a few nervous looks as I got strapped up, but what was the worst that could happen? I've got MND.

Others had travelled a very long way in their support of the Lions, to Australia, South Africa and particularly New Zealand, but had never seen the kind of performances and results that the Lions achieved in the summer of 2017.

Ever since I left the game of rugby as a player, I've realised there is no point in getting hung up or upset about scores. I say that because when you're not a player, there is nothing you can do about it. You enjoy the occasion. And the occasion that was the Lions being in New Zealand was just awesome.

You had two teams – one in black, one in red – and if you saw someone in red, be they Irish, English, Welsh or Scots, you went and said hello, where are you from, how are you getting on and do you know your way to the bar?

Even if there was a World Cup in South Africa, or a tour to Australia, for instance, other than a change of scenery, it isn't that different from being at Murrayfield or Twickenham for the Scots or English fans. You support your team and mix with your own.

But in New Zealand, they – the followers from all four nations, for the duration of that tour – were your own. Aye, even the English. Really, they were quite nice, and that's not to say that the people bedecked in black weren't nice. Our hosts, the people of New Zealand, were considerate and compassionate. They were lovely, very hospitable and generous.

But there was a time and a place to be nice and make new friends and a time when you stuck together with the Lions pack, particularly around the three Tests.

It was lovely meeting the Lions fans, hard at times to believe there were just so many of them halfway around the world. They were great towards me. I can't imagine how many selfies and photos I posed for during that tour. Every time you'd stop or turn, walk into a shop, or a pub, or a stadium, or another bar, there was always someone trying to grab you for a pic. And lovely it was.

It was funny, looking on the various social media apps and sites (always on someone else's phone given that mine was out of commission) where you could see the photographs that were taken during the morning, afternoon, at the beginning of the night, and those that were taken nearer close of play. Let's just say that my demeanour had changed somewhat, that I may have wilted a wee bit and, most certainly, that I looked a bit more rosy-cheeked.

I stand guilty as charged.

There was one night that I had a session with Craig Chalmers that left me wounded the next day. Who'd have thought that we could be 12,000 miles away, on one of our first nights in New Zealand, and Kathy and I out for something to eat, and the first person we walk into is Chick. It would have been rude not to catch up with someone who I like and know so well, and who I hadn't seen in a long time. Again, not easy in the circumstances, and emotional, but a few beers later, it was like the good old days. As Kathy, who left us to do what ex-teammates do on a night out, was quick to remind me the next morning.

The sheep farmers from Wales were there, the bankers from London, and the Irish crews, who had various ways of earning a living. There were boys and girls who had been saving up for four years, longer in some instances, just to be out there. Others just put everything on the credit card and worried about it later. But they all had an incredible time.

Kenny Logan, Phil Vickery and Brian O'Driscoll were among those I happened to stumble upon, great for my family to meet them, and it would have been rude not ask about their wellbeing, about their respective families, and how they thought the Lions would do. And before you know it, Kathy had vanished with the boys and I had spent another three hours chatting. Mary Doll was very understanding, and a very good driver of the campervan, of a morning, with me unconscious in the back. Ach, I was on tour.

Another night, in Wellington, we arrived at the Lions hotel and I met Rob Howley, who was on the Lions tour in 1997 with me, and indeed, the two of us came back on the 'ambulance' plane together from that tour. I had a really good long chat with him, and great to see him again.

On the way home, one of our pals from Hawick, Cammy Rudkin, spotted the All Blacks hotel. Why don't we have a nightcap? he suggested.

Just in the door, and there was Sean Fitzpatrick, Grant Fox, John Kirwan, Jeff Wilson and Steve Hansen. The kids got selfies with these legends, and I was able to speak to Jeff, whose brother Richard was diagnosed with MND. It is amazing just how many people have been touched in one way or another by this dreadful condition. However, seeing all these lads again was terrific. And they stood us a drink.

Even though I knew a lot of players out there, they all wanted their wee minute with me, to ask if I was okay, did I need anything, to tell me that they'd be there for me. It was nice but tough-going, especially when they looked you in the eye. But we knew that would be the measure of the folk we'd meet on the trip.

And the All Blacks were lovely. They were out doing their media and press interviews and grabbed the kids and our group to say hello and pose for photos and the likes. Remember, this was the day before the Test matches and it was great of them to take time out to do that. The kids loved it and, for once, actually appeared to be speechless at the experience. No back-chatting when you're with the All Blacks.

Samuel Whitelock, Sonny Bill Williams, Beauden Barrett, Dane Coles and captain Kieran Read – who I'd meet later in the year as well – all gave of their time ahead of some of the most important games of their career, just to make the boys and my family feel special. I will never forget that gesture.

The Lions, though, were immense. To lose the First Test in Auckland, bounce back in Wellington, and then draw 15–15 in the third and final Test to share the spoils was an amazing performance at Eden Park. I had been invited to participate in a hospitality function alongside Will Greenwood and former All Blacks Justin Marshall and Keven Mealamu. It was fantastic, with the people at Eden Park giving me a table for ten guests for the last Test, and Thomas – or Tam the Bam as he's affectionately known – and his family even managed to get into the posh seats for the game. It was just such a great way to round off a wonderful stay.

However, while the rugby and the occasions were amazing to experience and to watch, and being in and among the supporters was great, that wasn't the most important thing to me.

Sorry, I don't want that to sound as if I didn't appreciate the blood, sweat, tears and effort you must have shed to gain those results against the champions of the world. Well done to the Lions players and coaching staff. It was nice that you stepped up your game for me being out there and you made a great many people very happy and feeling that they'd spent their money wisely. The Lions tour management, meanwhile, also made me feel very honoured and humble with their assistance and kindness, especially when it came to sourcing tickets.

However, spending time away with my family was what really counted for me, way above the occasion. The trip gave me time with my brother Tom, something 'Ginger' and I hadn't shared for a while, mostly because we were involved with different clubs, me at Melrose and him at Gala, and therefore had our own circle of friends. Even though we both played rugby, and for two big teams, we were never that connected through rugby. New Zealand gave us time to make that connection, which was nice.

At the end of the trip, on the last night, we had a court session. Now, any rugby players out there, or anyone familiar with the Lions on tour will know about these court sessions. Basically, someone brings a charge against you, and you have to defend yourself against those allegations, and you have a judge who presides over events. But if you fail to bring someone to justice, you are the one who needs to do the forfeit.

The more outrageous the charge, the more chance you have of making it stick, usually, depending on the judge. I wasn't for being very lenient.

My nephew, Douglas, Tom's son, is only fifteen, and was being a bit gobby during the court proceedings. Of course, this was viewed as being contempt and therefore he needed to be punished.

What better than to make him down a couple of shots of Bundaberg Rum, an Aussie potion which my brother likes, possibly given his thrifty nature, because no one else will drink it, although other rums are available.

That shut him up, and probably put Douglas off rum for good. Don't see it as a punishment; view it instead as preventative medicine. Only time will tell if it worked. That and whether his dad's stock of Bundaberg evaporates.

New Zealand was just wonderful. There was Scott and Will and me on the 1997 Lions tour together and, twenty years later, meeting under entirely different circumstances. And bumping into Chick, who I'd toured New Zealand with twice, and Rob and those All Black greats, all friends forever through our wonderful game. All this, for me and my family, possible only through the generosity of one special individual. I will never forget that, much like the journey itself.

12

World Cups

D URING THE 2014 COMMONWEALTH GAMES I saw an article by the boxing world champion Nicola Adams, who said that her first two appearances at major championships, the 2012 Olympics in London and in Glasgow two years later, were trips she could have made on the bus. No globetrotting for her. And in some ways my exploits at the World Cup with Scotland were a lot like that.

Other than a memorable trip to South Africa in 1995, 1991 and 1999 were local to us. While we were playing in the World Cup – the biggest tournament in the game – in 1999 especially, I never really felt the excitement, or nerves, possibly because the surroundings were all too familiar, as were our final opponents in all of these tournaments, namely the All Blacks.

Being named in the squad for the 1991 World Cup was by no means a certainty. It was only a year before that I'd made my debut for Scotland, then sat through the Five Nations, but I had some of the senior players pushing for me to be included, as indeed they had been since the previous summer and the tour to New Zealand.

But imagine the thrill of your first major tournament and major involvement for your country, as a player, being a World Cup in the city where you once went to school. How good was that?

We had one warm-up match, losing in Bucharest to Romania. Not the planned outcome, but one that could be forgotten about before we kicked off our World Cup proper against the Japanese.

Fundamentally, Scotland went into that tournament with their Grand Slam-winning team plus two changes: me in for Damian Cronin, and hooker John Allan squeezing out Kenny Milne for that berth. There was even a recall for Finlay 'Sinatra' Calder, who had retired after the summer tour to New Zealand in 1990 but who Ian McGeechan had coaxed back for the World Cup.

The Japan game, won convincingly, was interesting because of who I ended up shoving. I'd packed down behind brothers Iain and Kenny Milne out in New Zealand the previous year, but now, like some kind of sticker collection, here was me with the full set when David trotted on as a replacement to win his first cap – or his only cap, as his siblings are quick to remind him.

Next up was Zimbabwe, for which several key players were rested. Not yet being a key player, I played and scored one of eight tries, Iwan Tukalo finishing off three of the others.

Our last group game against the Irish would decide who we would play in the quarter-finals, not that we were entirely sure who that might be. In the opening round of matches Western Samoa upset the draw – and Wales – when they scored a shock 16–13 win in Cardiff, a dark day for the Welsh which gave birth to the famous 'thank heavens we weren't playing the whole of Samoa' line.

With Murrayfield full, Ireland led 12–9 at half time, but we upped our game after the turnaround to win 24–15. Wales went out, losing to the Australians, with the Samoans overcoming Argentina. So, in beating the Irish, we avoided the Aussies, which meant Samoa at Murrayfield.

On paper, it was the ideal draw, but as the Welsh had found, this was a useful Samoan team, especially as, at that time, they could call on the services of Brian Lima, future All Blacks Frank Bunce and Stephen Bachop, and a new boy by the name of Pat Lam at number 8, winning only his third cap.

For want of a better description, we hit them with everything up front and, I think, broke their spirits. The back row of Jeffrey (who scored a brace of tries), Calder and Derek White was absolutely immense. Seeing it close up, you suddenly realised what these guys had both as a unit and individually and why they were Grand Slam winners and Lions.

And now it was on to the semi-final and who else but England. This would be my first appearance against England. It would eventually end like all the rest, in defeat.

There was nothing remarkable about the lead-up to the game, or the game itself. I know you would think – well, I did – that there would have been some reference to 1990, but that historic day, which I enjoyed as a fan, wasn't really mentioned. And if it was, it came with the line 'it won't be the same' joined on at the end. Why it wasn't made the same, I have no idea.

In years to come, I would be told – and would tell others – to enjoy the moment, leave everything on the field, and not be thinking afterwards about what you should have done, when you'd had the chance to do it for eighty minutes.

Even so, I couldn't tell you anything really about the match itself. JJ got to lead the team out on his last appearance at Murrayfield, an excellent gesture from captain David Sole.

I remember thinking during the match that I wasn't making any impression on Paul Ackford and Wade Dooley, daytime officers of the law, who I was playing opposite. They were anything but sleeping policemen. And those are about the only cogent memories I have of such an immensely important match.

Ironically, a few years later at Newcastle, the game came up in some chat with Rob Andrew, and he hadn't a clue what happened either, other than Gavin Hastings missing a penalty attempt.

He was one up on me! I have no live recollection of that kick or how it came about. None. Maybe I erased it from my memory on the sound of the final whistle. I assume there was a whistle.

What I do remember was the disappointment in the dressing room. It was like a morgue, other than the click of studs, and the usual moans when tape was being peeled off, or you found a knock you didn't know you had. There was no real chat. People just slumped, head in hands; the captain, Chick, Gary, JJ all looked washed out. Our World Cup was over, except it wasn't.

We had lost, but we were still in the tournament. As the losing semi-finalists, we had the consolation of getting to play for third place, against New Zealand, who had lost their semi to the Australians in Dublin.

But first we would need to recover properly, so Finlay wheeched everyone on to the team bus and took us out to Sighthill, where we all decanted into a local pub. Here was the Scotland team who had been on STV an hour before, still all blazered up, drinking with the locals who looked totally bemused by our arrival.

A day after the England match, we were on our way to Cardiff to face the Kiwis. We had never beaten the All Blacks. No pressure then.

From my perspective, there seemed to be a wee spring in the step again; people had come to, and we were looking forward to giving New Zealand a game. There was a bit more life about the camp, and I can only put that down to suddenly having all the shackles of expectation and focus removed, now that we were no longer in the tournament proper.

We could be more like our old selves, and maybe being more relaxed would help us against New Zealand.

When I came into the Scotland set-up, Kenny Milne and his wife Ellie, much the same as Chris Gray and his wife Jude, were really kind to me. I was still a pretty raw boy, albeit a big boy, and they looked after me. Mentoring is the modern description for the guys, or mothering as the ladies – or even some of the gentleman – among you might call it.

The mothering thing was about to get real for Judith. She was expecting, due imminently, and indeed gave birth that week, which was something else that brought some normality to proceedings, except I suspect for new dad Chris.

Preparations for the midweek game were quite light, walks and gentle runs, allowing us to rest up. There was then a bit of spare time.

I'd always fancied myself as a bit of a cueist. The reality was I would have struggled with a bus queue, never mind a pool or snooker cue. But I was keen, and most camps or hotels had a pool table as another activity to break the monotony of hotel life. It seemed a good idea to challenge Kenny Milne to a game of pool. I mean, he was a hooker, and I'd seen his hand-eye coordination at many a line-out, so I fancied my chances.

Being last of the big spenders, I asked if he wanted to play for a pound, and duly lost it.

'Double or quits?'

'Aye, if you want,' said Kenny, offering me the chance to break again.

I potted one, then another, but Kenny still won that frame as well.

'Double or quits?'

'Fine,' replied Kenny, breaking off and grannying me. (In other words, I didn't pot a ball.)

'Double or quits?'

Would Kenny buy it? Of course he would.

Anyway, I was four grand down when Kenny decided he'd had enough of playing pool, telling me that it didn't matter about the money, thankfully. I was only good for a tenner really.

This match was the first time I'd faced the All Blacks

and, therefore, the first time I'd been confronted by the Haka. We faced up to it, but it did sod all good – a bit like every other tactic we used. I even once told Ian Jones his willy was hanging out of his shorts. He didn't take kindly to that.

The game itself was swung by Walter Little's try in favour of New Zealand, but the highlight belonged to the Scots, when Gavin, on the charge, just ran through the All Blacks prop Richard Loe. It literally happened straight in front of me, and for a split second I had to question in my own mind what I'd just witnessed. It was like something out of a Tom and Jerry cartoon.

The match ended 13–6 for New Zealand, and it was the end for Finlay, JJ and Chris with Scotland. Me, I'd enjoyed getting to face the All Blacks for the first time and going toe to toe with Gary Whetton and Ian Jones, not to mention Michael Jones and Zinzan Brooke. It was also a chance to see someone who would become a teammate in later years, one Inga Tuigamala in action.

We had a beer or several that night after the New Zealand play-off, and after a month of rugby, we deserved it. Of course, there was still the final to be played at Twickenham, England against Australia, and quite a few of us managed to procure tickets.

It was well publicised at the time that some of the Scotland team (who will remain nameless) supported the Aussies rather than England, even going to the length of wearing gold and green scarves. I can say categorically I was not one of them.

I had a hat.

★

Four years on and we were all headed for South Africa and what was only the third ever World Cup, which came almost directly after the domestic season finished in the UK. Scotland had a great Five Nations, only losing out to England for the Grand Slam, and I really felt we carried that momentum into the World Cup, which out of the three I played in, was probably my favourite.

There was a relaxed feeling to proceedings. Yes, there had been all sorts of scare stories about occurrences out in the streets in various places in South Africa, but within the squad, we were in a good place and, under head coach Dougie Morgan, there was a more relaxed feel.

First game up we scored thirteen tries, which was unlucky for Ivory Coast as we won 89–0, with big Gav scoring four tries in a personal haul of forty-four points. He was on the bell in the bar that night.

As I've always said, I treat everyone the same, which means on many occasions I have quickly bonded with people that maybe we weren't supposed to come into contact with. That seemed to be particularly true of policemen, and by that I mean the friendly sort, not arresting officers.

In South Africa, during the World Cup, Pieter the Policeman, one of our security detail, decided to take us for a drive in his police car, just to let me see what his normal beat looked like, around some of the townships. Had I followed the rules and protocols, I would never have witnessed that. It was something I'll never forget, for all the wrong reasons.

Never had I seen anything like it, people squeezed on top of more people, their houses nothing more than lean-tos, which, if you came across something like that on your farm, you'd pull down. Out in the townships, you could have a dozen or fifteen people living in one.

It was an eye opener, especially when we returned to the hotel, to the affluent accommodation we had during a tournament that, ultimately, was selling South Africa to the world.

And it succeeded. Because, to my mind, there has never been a more emotional, political or iconic sporting photograph than there was at the end of the final, when Nelson Mandela, wearing a Springbok number 6 shirt, presented the World Cup to the man who played in the number 6 Springbok shirt, Francois Pienaar.

But we were still a bit off that action when we played and beat Tonga, which took us to our last group game and a clash with France to decide who the opposition would be in the quarter-final. A win, and we would play Ireland at Newlands, the winners probably guaranteed a semi-final tie against South Africa in a rainy Durban. I'd have fancied our chances in that.

Instead, somehow, referee Wayne Erickson found four minutes of injury time and we lost to the French, Emile Ntamack going over in the corner for a try in the dying seconds.

My first experience of defeat in the World Cup was that semi-final against England, when the atmosphere in the changing room really was like death warmed up. After losing to the French, though, there was real upset, anger and resentment. Firstly, because we should have won it, and, secondly, because of the manner in which we lost the game.

I'm not saying there were grown men close to tears, but it was a bitter loss for those who would be retiring from international rugby at the end of the tournament.

We had a full week to get ready for the quarter-final, so a trip to MalaMala Game Reserve had been planned in advance, just to give us a break from the intensity of the rugger. We flew east and into the jungle in something like an old DC3. This wasn't your Edinburgh Zoo. As soon as we got off the plane and into the Land Rovers, the ground staff on the airstrip began covering the aircraft wheels up with thorny bushes.

'It's the best way to stop the hyenas eating the rubber,' we were told. And I thought foxes pinching chickens was bad.

There were dancers there to welcome us, and we were all billeted into our cabins. Because it was so quiet at night every noise was amplified. Imagine what it sounded like when a troop of baboons decided to go for a run through the camp.

They weren't the only things making a noise. The lions almost looked trained to roar when any vehicles passed by. What they hadn't expected was Kenny Logan roaring back at them, and getting them all a bit frisky.

This was normal behaviour for Kenny. When he'd come and stay with me on the farm, he'd wake up in the morning, lift the window, and start shouting at the cows. We put it down to him not getting out very much.

We returned to base after a couple of days to plot how

we were going to stop the All Blacks or, more precisely, one man.

Jonah Lomu had taken the World Cup by storm. There were plenty of players who were six foot five and nearly nineteen stone, but none I knew of that could run one hundred metres in eleven seconds. It might have been 10.7 actually. But did it matter? With that pace and athleticism, and bulk, he could have a devastating effect on any defensive line.

Craig Joiner was the man directly opposed to Lomu. But we weren't just going to leave it to my wee fellow Melrosian to stop him. We had two tactics to employ. One: stop the ball getting near Lomu. And two: cramp him for space if he did get it and basically get as many numbers on him as possible.

But that was, of course, easier said than done, and Lomu set up New Zealand's first score having rumbled through several road blocks. He would score himself, but we did contain him, certainly better than England would do the following week.

Unfortunately, the All Blacks had fantastic players throughout and stopping them was just as difficult. But we gave it a go, especially early on. Our backs – and there were four from Melrose in the team – took the game to the All Blacks, and the mobility of our pack really was getting the better of them in the loose.

I've often wondered what would have happened had we taken a more measured three points on offer from a penalty in front of the sticks when 7–6 behind, rather than a speedy but profitless quick tap.

We were down by 17–9 at the interval, then New Zealand

upped their game early in the second half, stretching out to 31–9 before yours truly spun off a rolling maul and over for a try. There was a half side-step in there as well, but the cameras just didn't catch it.

That riled the All Blacks who clocked up another fourteen unanswered points before I scored again. This time their scrum-half Graeme Bachop messed up a clearance kick, Eric Peters managed to divert the ball back, and I picked up to drive over with the rest of the pack in tow.

Scott Hastings also touched down for a score, but while we gave a great account of ourselves in what was a fantastic game to play in – and a lot of that was down to the referee, Derek Bevan of Wales – we had lost again to New Zealand at a third successive World Cup. Some day – maybe next time.

With that, having let our hair down post-match, we packed our bags ready for the off.

Back home, rather than thoughts of putting our feet up, there appeared to be some substance around what had been rumours of a professional 'rebel' competition being set up across the world involving thirty teams, driven out of Australia, and involving mainly players from there, New Zealand and South Africa, with a team in Scotland.

Gavin Hastings was the recruiter-in-chief, with a three-year deal worth £120,000 per annum. Where do I sign?

Professionalism was coming, but I would still believe it when I saw it, regardless of how many bits of paper had my signature on them. Then the South Africans reneged and it all evaporated. Except the International Rugby Board had been given a real wake-up call. Professionalism would come and the IRB wanted to call the shots.

By the time the next World Cup came around, pro rugby was fully established, even if there was still the odd skirmish and fallout between clubs, owners and individual nations.

★

There was a bit of positivity and razzmatazz about the 1999 World Cup, which apparently was being staged in Wales, even if we played all of our matches at Murrayfield. Talk about a home from home, or was it déjà vu?

The positivity came from what we – I say 'we' in the loosest possible terms given my forty-minute contribution – had managed in the Five Nations Championship that spring. Maybe not enough to put money on us as possible winners (unless you were an easily impressed M1 traffic cop – more of which later . . .), but sufficient to believe we were more than capable of making it to at least the last eight.

Meanwhile, the buzz around the tournament came from certain stunts devised to help generate more of an atmosphere during games, seriously required given the attendances at some of the ties we were involved in, even at Murrayfield.

One of the things they tried was playing music after each try scored, individually selected by the player in advance of the tournament. At the time, I was contracted to write a column for the *Scottish Mirror*, so when it came to choosing my celebration song, I picked (actually it was done for me) the Human League and, you might have guessed it, 'Mirror Man'.

How corny. Actually, it was quite clever, especially as I

fancied my chances of getting on the scoreboard, particularly with the level of opponent in some of the games, although maybe not the first.

The way the tournament was drawn, both in terms of the group section and the resultant play-off and knockout stages, we always knew that the first game was key against South Africa.

As a squad, we had gone out to the Cape for a mini-tour, playing four provincial sides – Border, Northern Free State, Pumas and Golden Lions – in preparation for the big event, winning two and losing the last two. It gave us something of an insight into what we might face when we came up against the Springboks but, ultimately, it was more to keep us in a state of readiness for the World Cup.

Against the defending World Cup holders in our opening tie, we bagged a sizeable tally of points, but still lost 43–29.

From that point it was pretty much certain that for a fourth successive tournament – and, remember, at that point in history there had only ever been four competitions – we were going to face favourites New Zealand come the quarter-finals.

The next two matches were where I fancied grabbing a try or two, as I did against the All Blacks four years before, something I seldom mention. First up were Uruguay, and while we conceded forty-three points against the Boks, that's what we helped ourselves to against the South Americans. Unfortunately I didn't play. However, I returned against Spain, a 48–0 win, me and Andy Reed together in the second row, but alas no tries for me in that one either.

When you start with five group sections – in other words,

an odd number – all thanks to the expansionist plans within world rugby, you know that getting down to eight quarter-finalists is going to be an arithmetic conundrum. Therefore we ended up with a play-off tie against Samoa, me squaring up to my Falcons pals Pat Lam and Inga Tuigamala.

We won 35–20, which was convincing, but less convincing was the buy-in from the spectators. Playing on a Wednesday afternoon, only 15,000 watched the game. With a 67,000 capacity, a quarter full (or three-quarters empty) Murrayfield was just a giant echo chamber. No problems with not hearing line-out calls, though. Nevertheless, it was job done, although I still hadn't earned any royalties for Phil Oakey. New Zealand awaited, as did our orange change kit.

I didn't mind it too much, but some of the other guys really detested it. As it transpired, our future was neither bright nor orange, and the Kiwis turned us over by 30–18. Out wide, New Zealand murdered us: Jonah Lomu scoring a touchdown, fellow winger Tana Umaga scoring a brace.

Stuart Grimes had replaced me and, with that, my World Cup was over.

Australia, just as they had eight years earlier, won the final in Cardiff, beating the French who had turned in a mesmeric display in the semi-finals to overturn New Zealand. On this occasion however, my Aussie hat stayed at home, like me.

But, when I left the field against the All Blacks, it meant my days with Scotland were at an end, although I didn't think or realise that at the time. I was still only twenty-nine. Surely still time to squeeze another tournament in, come 2003 in Australia. Or so I thought, a bit like I had believed this World Cup malarkey was a breeze when I played a semi-final as a twenty-one-year-old against England back in 1991.

Alas, circumstances, most of them beyond my control, were to rule out another World Cup.

It had been good fun, getting to play in three tournaments when some players had been lucky to manage one, and other greats of the Scottish game, none at all.

My record tally of appearances for Scotland in the World Cup, fourteen, was eventually surpassed by Chris Paterson, who took four tournaments to better my total, and only beat it in his final game against England in New Zealand in 2011 while winning his 109th Scotland cap. That's a helluva lot of miles to put on the clock – both in terms of air and physical – just to lead by one. But well done, the only disappointment being the record now belongs to a Gala man.

But I'll rewind before I end this chapter, back to 1991 and 1995.

After the England game, such was the emotion after the hammer blow of losing, that I never watched so much as a news bulletin that might contain any footage of the match. Why would I? It was showing a team celebrating and going to the final, a team that wasn't mine.

Therefore, it really was only very recently – and it might have been during the last World Cup – that I hit upon Gavin missing that kick against England, pulling it to the right of the posts from no more than about twenty-five metres out. And having seen it, finally, I now realise why Chick looked so shocked and gaunt.

Now, after the pain of that loss has subsided, twenty-seven years on, I only have one thing to say to Gavin.

'Gavin, what were you doing?'

Four years later, and Gavin had announced his retirement after our great South African World Cup adventure, and as I have mentioned earlier, was acting recruitment sergeant for a possible jump into professional rugby.

Reflecting on that, while putting these words together, two things strike you.

First, pre-1995, and the amateur game, feels like a different world. No less important to pride and spirit, but so much more easy-going and relaxed.

The second one is that I – we – were part of the biggest seismic change to impact on rugby union in its history, namely adopting professionalism. I've never seen myself as any kind of maverick, or groundbreaker. But that was the role we were about to be cast in, just by being one of the first to try and make a living from playing our sport. What could be wrong with that?

13

Leaving Melrose

THE COMING OF THE PROFESSIONAL era meant it was a good time to be a top-grade rugby player, but a tricky time as well.

By that I mean I have always been pretty loyal to people and done what I considered the decent thing, whether it was with office bearers, teammates, clubs, sponsors and the likes. I'd imagine others would have been pretty much the same, playing for their hometown club, or where they studied or moved to through work.

Without sounding too goody-goody, I have tried to treat people the way I would want to be treated. It hasn't always worked out; sometimes it hasn't been very pleasant. But, on the whole, I've always believed it was the proper way to go about things.

That said, there may have been a bit of naivety starting out in the big new professional world, because compared to the amateur game, different rules applied and that meant different standards, for some. That player–town–club relationship, quite literally, was going to change forever.

Things were never going to be the same ever again. It never is when money is introduced into the equation, and no one knew what things were going to be like once they had changed. It was all a hypothetical guessing game.

If that sounds confusing, it's because at the time it was entirely that. Adopting professionalism was one thing, but the majority of people were in the dark as to how that professionalism was to be structured. It was as if we'd be amateur on the Saturday, and then professional come the Monday. And someone would put money in our account at the end of the week. That simple? It wasn't.

I had come out of college with an HND in agriculture – I know, I seldom talk about it, mainly because it would mean giving credit to all my mates who allowed me to copy their work – David Ireland and Hamish Dykes in particular. But, despite having this much-envied qualification, because I was playing for Melrose – and more importantly in terms of being away, playing for Scotland – and with all the time rugby was taking up, my old boy didn't want me back on the farm. Some would say his judgement was sound, me being one of them.

He didn't think there would be enough work for us, which was a kinder and more thoughtful way of saying I wouldn't have been doing enough work had I been there. That meant, armed with my HND, seeking a full-time job doing something other than agriculture. This would be in 1992.

Primarily through the connection with Melrose and the Calder's beer brand, I landed a job with Carlsberg Tetley Alloa, and what a job that was. Pub lunches every day, a game of darts, a game of pool. Fantastic. What a working day. And I even had a sponsored car from Dalgleish Nissan, with Scott Dalgleish, a Gala man, taking care of the Melrose boy. To balance things up, Gregor Townsend got one as well.

Maybe it wasn't up there with the one Kenny Logan had, a Mondeo, all fancy wings and side skirts, top of the range, with 'Kenny Logan, Stirling County and Scotland, proudly sponsored by Fergusson Coal' on the side. The rest of us were trying to keep up with him.

Thinking about it, that Nissan wasn't my first 'sponsored' car. I was given a second-hand Cavalier, with someone kindly writing on the side, 'Sponsored by Doddie's Dad'.

But all in all, life was pretty good as a rugby player then. Why would you ever want to become a professional?

Actually, there were a few reasons. One being the money was a bit better; the other was, the way rugby was going, you'd need to be full-time to keep playing with Scotland; and, lastly, you wanted to try yourself out against the very best, week in, week out.

There had been some chat about professionalism during the summer of 1995, when we were away with Scotland at the World Cup, all of it speculation, or conjecture, or just stuff that had been made up then passed on as fact.

Truth was no one knew how it would come about; would it be a gradual process, fed in over a year, or quicker? As it transpired, quite literally it took place either side of midnight one evening. As quick as that.

Needless to say, you couldn't have a conversation with anyone involved in rugby without 'the future' appearing on the agenda. I don't think I've ever heard such knowledgeable and convincing tittle-tattle. Seriously, because there was no direction, no blueprint, no business plan to work from, the more bizarre the scenario of who would be paid and, more importantly, where the money would come from, the more believable and plausible it all became.

In the real world, minus the contracts and pound signs, we were back playing rugby and into a new season, 1995/96, with our clubs. It was all change in terms of our schedule as well. The regular league season would run from the start of the season until December, and then at the turn of the year it was into inter-district rugby, the new European club competitions, and the Five Nations.

In the league, Melrose's form was a bit up and down, and ironically one of those downs came at Mansfield Park, where we lost 10–9 to Hawick. I never liked losing – or the reception you would get in Melrose for the rest of the week or until you put it right. They loved their rugby, were proud of their team, and were opinionated regardless. Probably no different in those traits to countless other local teams across these islands.

Then Ian McLauchlan, the former Scotland captain and now a player agent, rang and said Rob Andrew would like to speak to me. The newly appointed Newcastle director of rugby/stand-off Rob Andrew?

'Is this a wind up?'

You couldn't be too careful, given some of the comedians I knew. But it was genuine, because not only was I about to make the journey, I'd be in the company of a certain Gary Armstrong, who'd also received the 'pop in for a cuppa' call.

It was maybe not a bad week then to head over Hadrian's Wall for a wee sniff around the all-new professional set-up at Gosforth, or Newcastle Falcons as it would eventually be known. The newspapers were full of Peter Wright's pending suspension after his sending-off during Boroughmuir's win against Gala (which gave them a three-point lead in the championship), and with the Scotland team for the Test against Western Samoa being announced, 'AN Other' was at tight head while Wrighty awaited his fate.

Gary and myself were teammates in the Scotland side, and occasionally with the South, but that was really as close as we were. He was rugby royalty compared to me: OBE, in every Hall of Fame that had been opened, retired, then got to make a comeback, all because I put a ball on a plate for him for years. He has never said thank you either.

Anyway, it was Rob who put the two of us together, on our first date, the 'Odd Couple', so we decided to go for a look about the place, just to see what Newcastle was all about and if we liked the sound of this professionalism thing. We really were that much in the dark about this new venture, but what a wonderful feeling to even be invited, considered, by Mr Andrew.

Gary and me drove down to St James' Park, home of Newcastle United, which the rugby club would come to use occasionally for training, and used to impress would-be recruits. What could possibly go wrong?

Next thing, us pair ended up sitting at one end of a table, at a press conference, with Tony Underwood sitting at the other, in the process of signing for the Falcons from Leicester.

A quiet recce? A wee nosey about? A visit to see what was on offer?

I looked at Gary. He didn't have to say anything. He looked utterly gobsmacked, like a rabbit in headlights. So I must have looked like a giant rabbit in headlights. Then Gary mouthed a four-letter expletive, beginning with 'f', followed by, 'How did this happen?' Remember what I said about naivety?

In his book, Rob Andrew says I called him a 'bastard'. I don't remember. If I did, he got away lightly. Neither does Gary remember much. Rabbits have extremely bad memories.

But maybe, just maybe, it would be seen by the assembled press as nothing more than a fact-finding mission for Gary and me. Aye, that was possible, an entirely plausible explanation.

On the way back up the road, coming across the Carter Bar, we picked up Radio Borders again, and their sports bulletin at half past whatever hour it was on a very long day, broadcast to the world – well, our world – that two Scotland international players from the Borders were set to turn professional with Newcastle.

Maybe no one heard it? Aye, that was possible. Maybe there was another two players there that we just didn't see?

Next day, the story was splashed across the newspapers, even the tabloids that seldom did anything on rugby beyond internationals. It appeared this was a story, supplemented by phrases like 'cash in', 'reaping rewards' and 'gravy train'. Maybe no one read them?

The cat was very much out the bag, but that was always

going to happen. We just wanted to be able to tell people in advance, rather than them finding out second-hand, through media reports, which goes back to what I said earlier about staying loyal to folk. Formal contracts hadn't been agreed, never mind signed, but we had signed registration forms. There was nothing unusual in that. I'd done exactly the same for the previous two years, with West Hartlepool. It's called keeping all your options open.

Meantime, my 'real job' boss while I was working for Carlsberg Tetley Alloa was a chap called Bill McRandle and he was fantastic. He'd helped me a lot – and put up with even more – while I worked with him and the business.

It was only right that I explained everything to Bill, about my options and what I was thinking, and long before I'd made any firm decision, never mind commitment.

He just said, 'Look, son, go for it,' and that it was the chance of a lifetime. Maybe he wanted to get rid of me, a bit like my dad on the farm. Nah, I don't think that was the case. But he was very good about it and calmed some of my fears and apprehensions by telling me the beer trade would always be here for me, whereas the Newcastle offer – or similar elsewhere – might not come again. And that was that.

Newcastle appeared a logical choice for me in a non-rugby sense. It wasn't a million miles away from 'home' (not even a hundred, being pedantic) and I had started dating a lass from Northumberland (you'll have read more on her elsewhere). I've always believed as well that you should give everything a try at least once. That way you get to be the judge, no one else, and you don't need to live with any regrets in the future.

The more time I spent considering the prospect, the more I went from 'will I, won't I?' to 'I will'.

Still, we were happy. And I was happy for Gary. He was a bit older, twenty-eight at the time, and he'd been given a great chance of earning something from the game, having given so much for Jed-Forest and Scotland.

Our joy wasn't universally shared, however.

While Gary had limited success with his club, compared to what he'd achieved for country, I was very much the opposite. Melrose were the dominant force in the Scottish club scene at that time and had been for several seasons prior to rugby going through this major transformation. And I had been a key part of it. That's not being big headed or anything. Doing the business for Melrose got me into the Scotland team and meant that the movers and shakers at Newcastle got to see me against the best. But, first and foremost, I was a Melrose man.

My teammates, Hoggy (Carl Hogg), Brush (Bryan Redpath), Chick (Craig Chalmers), Graham Sheil, Robbie Brown, all of them and the rest, were delighted, chuffed for me and wished me all the best. They recognised the chance I was being given and knew this was the future of rugby. A few of them would have known they too could be faced with an identical decision soon.

I thanked them then and would still reiterate those thanks now. Without them, I would never have been offered a contract of that nature. It was testament to how good they were as a team that I got my chance to turn pro. Similarly, with the work Jim Telfer put in at the Greenyards, and Rob Moffat. And what a great time we had winning. You can be a great player, but in rugby you win nothing on your own. And I still had ambitions, one being to win the league title again.

The season, which began late for me after missing pre-season and the first six weeks after a leg operation, was coming to an exciting conclusion. Hawick did us a turn by beating Boroughmuir, while we defeated Watsonians the same day, and then captain Bryan Redpath burrowed over for a match-clinching try, four minutes into stoppage time, against Edinburgh Accies. After the Autumn Test, we came from 15–0 down in the second half to draw with Stirling County. While Boroughmuir and Watsonians were in the mix, County were our main rivals for the crown.

Our last match was against relegated Gala, and the press made plenty of the fact that I'd be up against my brother Tom. We spoke about giving Gala the utmost respect, and how Thomas and me would be the best of enemies for eighty minutes, and friends afterwards. It filled the column inches.

I was nowhere near fully fit, and because of that I hadn't played as well as I could. But everything I had was going into that last tie. There was no way Tom, Gala or anyone else was going to have the pleasure of denying us the title.

We won 31–11, but didn't win the championship. Well, not immediately.

Stirling County could pip us, having one more match to play, but would have to beat Heriot's by forty-three points. That game wouldn't be for a fortnight, ample time for the champagne to chill. When the title decider was played out, County won but only by twenty points.

Even though we'd lost that same day in a Border League game at home to Selkirk, it was still time to celebrate winning the league title, our fifth in seven seasons. It had been hard going, arguably my most difficult, first having missed so much of the early part while recovering from surgery, then playing when down on fitness, and over the latter weeks, having to contend with the questions and quips – 'Are you still here?' – about what the future held for me.

With the title bagged, there had to be a resolution to my circumstances.

Unfortunately, while I had given a lot to help the team, there was less of the giving coming back the way. The whole business around professionalism appeared to bypass some, either because they didn't get it, or because they chose to entirely ignore the imminent changes, thinking it was just a fad and that it would go away.

In effect, Melrose tried to stall my move to Newcastle.

Did I understand that hostility? No, not really.

Professionalism was the right way to go, rather than what was ongoing. There were rumours about players already being paid, with the infamous tales of 'boot money', or people being given jobs as business development managers at building societies when the reality was they couldn't count their loose change, or at a different level, claiming petrol money and fuel receipts when you didn't even have a licence. There were dodgy dealings at play.

I had been amateur, other than the lovely perks you would get like flights – business class only for us freaks – hotels, king-sized beds no less, and the trips and the likes with Scotland. But you had achieved a very high standard to be a

Scotland player. I always thought those kind of perks were deserved, and had been earned.

Oh, I forgot our allowance, the spending money you got on tours. I once called it pocket money, which was frowned upon. And rightly so. I earned much more as a kid out of pocket money.

Joking aside, to maintain rugby's integrity, and be even-handed, and to bring it on to a level playing field with other team sports, professionalism was the route to go down.

There was an issue when the professional game came in, and I think a bit of a panic measure to stop the soon-to-be amateur teams missing out, with a ruling being tossed around that in order to turn pro, you had to have been with a club for the six months prior, or if changing to a club in another country, resident for a hundred and eighty days in that country.

When they tried to introduce it – that would be in February 1996 – Newcastle objected, and Sir John Hall had the solicitors lined up to fight it if necessary. This was where I first heard the name 'Bosman': a Belgian footballer around that time who had challenged the rules over transfers and freedom of contract. That name would mean more to me in a different context later, of course.

With regard to my circumstances, however, I was able to show I had been living with Kathy's family in Northumberland since the previous June, which was accepted by the English RFU. Our point was that we had signed registration documentation prior to this legislation being introduced, and subject to full terms being agreed, so the rule they were bringing in was retrospective to what we had actually done.

The International Rugby Board said they agreed – we understand what you've done, where you are and what you are up to – but it wasn't their call, and that we should go back to our member unions, which in our case meant the Scottish Rugby Union, housed at Murrayfield, and make our case with them.

To be fair, the SRU didn't have an issue either. I know the governing bodies and the establishment figures like the SRU get a bit of grief every now and again, and back then they did, being called out of touch and old fuddy-duddies.

But they were switched on, especially secretary Bill 'Boss' Hogg, to the notion of the professional game and, especially, where they wanted to be when the dust settled. There was no reason for the SRU to object and the RFU had no issue as I was covered by residency. Newcastle and ourselves played to the rules that were in place at the time. Those at Murrayfield looked at it plainly, in black and white, and made their call. As far as they read it, we were free to do what we liked. But the one stipulation was that we should have the blessing of our club, in my case Melrose.

Jed-Forest said to Gary good luck, you're one of us, come back and see us, we're always here, door is always open, enjoy it. Don't forget either that his dad, Lawrence, was the Jed president. But while Gary was waved away, certain individuals within Melrose didn't see it that way. That annoyed me. It wasn't going to benefit anyone and put Melrose at odds with me, and Newcastle, and the SRU and the RFU and the IRB. It might also have put them up against Newcastle's solicitors. For me, it was an almighty mess. What did they think they'd gain out of it, just by being different?

They just didn't want any players to be leaving Melrose, which, to an extent, I could understand. But they could never halt that progress across the game, across the world. Other clubs, much bigger than Melrose, in England, in Wales, in France, gave up the fight because it couldn't be won. The drive towards professionalism had so much momentum, and what went on in the club rooms at the Greenyards was never going to slow that.

We were the first of a generation, a new generation. No one had been here before. Had it happened ten years earlier, then some great players, some legends of Scottish rugby, might have benefited and got so much of what they put in to the game, back out. However, nothing was in place at that time to secure or guarantee them that.

Speaking to those players now, the 1990 Grand Slam winners for instance, while the money would be nice, I don't think any of them are particularly envious or jealous. They had their time, and I was about to have mine.

All it meant was that having had a very successful Five Nations with Scotland, and having played another Grand Slam game against England for a second successive year (they beat us, then Ireland, to take the title and the Triple Crown), I left Melrose on a bit of a sour note. Not what I would have wanted.

Given what has transpired since, for me, there is a bit of hypocrisy and irony evident over the 1995/96 season: an example of do what we say, not what we might do ourselves in the future.

Finally, on 23 March 1996, I made my Newcastle debut, alongside Rob, Gary and Tony, against Stirling County. All that hassle and hurt just to play wee Kevin McKenzie again!

Still, there was no point in using up my energies being upset then. I had a bigger adventure to come, and a bigger challenge ahead. And, on reflection, it's exactly the same today.

At Melrose, right across the club and the town, I've had so much to thank them for, and I see it to this day, with all the help, support, love, call it what you will.

When we launched the Trust and announced we'd be setting up the Foundation, we did it at the Greenyards. When we announced Doddie'5 Ride, we did it at Melrose. The club and myself did a joint dinner – with Jim Telfer, Chick, Gary, Stewart as MC and Jack Clark as auctioneer – at Prestonfield House, to help my charities and raise money for their new pitch and facilities.

What I feel for Melrose has never left me, and I think the vast majority of those around the club have always thought the same way. During that spell in the late 1980s and early 1990s, we were good for each other.

As for the rest, water under the bridge and all that ...

14

Newcastle Falcons Take Flight

THE WORLD CUP IN SOUTH AFRICA was over and done with. However, memories of the Springboks famously lifting the trophy in the company of Nelson Mandela were now being overtaken by events across the rugby world, namely, the introduction of professionalism, which was the reason we were about to pitch up at Newcastle Falcons.

Newcastle was a club built from nothing. That isn't strictly true. There was the passion from Sir John Hall, not just to make Newcastle Falcons the best rugby team in Britain, maybe even Europe, but to make the rugby team an integral part of his bigger vision to turn the North East, and especially Newcastle, into a hugely successful sporting hub, be that through us, Newcastle United, basketball or ice hockey. I think there was even a GT car – a Lister Storm – that ran in Newcastle United colours.

Sir John Hall wanted Newcastle and the surrounding area on the sporting map, and, in terms of rugby, he had an extremely efficient lieutenant in Rob Andrew.

There had been rugby clubs in the area before the Falcons,

like Northern, and Gosforth, which Newcastle basically took over. Scottish rugby fans will recognise the name as this was the club where the likes of Duncan Madsen and 'Lucky' Jim Pollock played, as had Lions Roger Uttley and Peter Dixon.

They had been an extremely good team during the 1970s. Then it was gone or, more accurately, absorbed. There was a bit of animosity that Gosforth's singular identity – for a season they'd be Newcastle Gosforth – had disappeared. I could understand that. The club and its history was being consigned to the past, and the players who'd played week in, week out, were being replaced by, for want of a better description – because we heard it and witnessed it – 'these mercenaries'.

Us big boys, however, drip-fed into the new set-up over the course of a year, had a sympathy and an empathy with the Gosforth guys. We had all played for smaller clubs, we all were loyal to those clubs, and we all worked for a living. We weren't as ruthless as to ignore how people might feel.

I think all concerned would have liked there to have been another way of doing things, but there wasn't really. There was a bit of upset. But the upset was across rugby, remember. No one said introducing a professional code was going to be easy, or smooth.

But most of those who came in were a wee bit older, and experienced, and knew that this might not be an opportunity that would be around for long, and that we might not get it again. Sentiment wasn't going to deny us the possibility of making a career of this rugby lark. It hasn't played out that way, and rugby at all levels has gone from strength to strength. But right at the outset, no one had a clue how things would pan out.

Let's not forget either, that in that first year, Newcastle owed a real debt to those who were already there. Richard 'Too Tall' Metcalfe, a man who made me look short, played alongside prop Paul Van Zandvliet – 'Tankie', who is sadly no longer with us – and Richard Arnold, a rough and ready flanker, along with Martin Wilson and Steve O'Neill. In that 1995/96 season, Newcastle could afford just about anything, bar one – relegation. Avoiding that was all-important and, despite a few scares, they remained in the second tier, ready to launch the big assault on promotion in the following campaign as Newcastle Falcons were launched on the world.

What replaced the old club at Gosforth was going to be something very special. And what replaced the amateur rugby ethos was every bit as much of a transformation.

Remember, for me, the switch to Newcastle came five years into my international career, even longer in terms of the club game, and I thought I was a pretty fit specimen, lean and mean. I was, in reality, a deluded eejit.

There was none of this 'doing your own thing'. Everything was regimented, laid out, set out and, above all else, adhered to.

The first weight session they gave us, we were working with these massive six kilo to eight kilo dumbbells, which was just ridiculous. Your ten-year-old son or daughter could probably throw them around. And there we were, at the end of the session, unable to put our arms up to wipe the sweat from our forehead.

Suddenly those games of pool and darts were being fondly remembered. *What is this hell I've let myself in for?* I don't know how many times I ended up with shampoo in my eyes because I had no energy left to reach the top of my head.

I kept thinking, *I should be better than this*. And then you remembered the times when you saw someone quite nice coming in to the gym in Galashiels, and you'd take the pin out the machine and knock the bar down ten or fifteen kilos just so you'd look a bit better – and then you wouldn't move it back because it felt a bit easier.

At Newcastle, there was no way of moving the pin, not when you had a personal trainer like Steve Black standing over you making sure everything was done properly, with the right amount of weight on board and the proper number of reps. You felt after a session as if someone had pulled your pin and you had just exploded – except you didn't have enough energy left to explode.

I hated training, pre- or mid-season. It progressively got more difficult, in terms of the levels of fitness and speed that had to be achieved. It is quite amazing how I was never caught, but every year I would be the best pupil when it came to improvement in fitness levels. During the season, you'd always have your fitness levels measured, be it with Melrose, Scotland or Newcastle, so you always knew it was going to happen.

Pre-season, July and August, you had the dreaded bleep test to contend with. I'd start slowly, with a ten, measured to perfection, so that with no additional work, I could push it up to eleven, twelve, even thirteen or a fourteen for good measure. Where did Dodgy Weir start? On ten – oh, he's really been putting the work in. Pass marks for another year.

I do, however, sometimes wonder what would have happened had I been a more dedicated trainer. But then you see the guys, magnificent physical specimens, who can run all day and bench press 300 pounds no bother, but who struggle to catch the ball or pass off their left hand.

For me there was fitness and strength, and then there was match fitness and strength. One was measurable on a scale; the other was only measurable on performances and results on the pitch. Which one do you remember twenty years into your retirement?

All of that said, Steve was amazing in what he did for me, and everyone else. I bulked up, with muscle, but still kept my speed and dexterity. Perhaps there was something in it, after all. I'd say there was a sadistic streak in Blackie if I could spell it. And, at the outset, his one-on-one involvement was just such a culture shock. But then that could be said of many things at the Falcons around then. The player recruitment was similarly bewildering.

The list of 'big boys' hired was quite astounding. Indeed, I was the only one I hadn't heard of. As the year went on, more new faces arrived, each one hand-picked.

I had sat in dressing rooms, at club and international level, and you'd look around knowing that maybe someone was the only person you had in that position, or that you were a tad light on reserves or replacements. But, as the 1996/97 season was played out, that didn't apply to the Falcons. We began to look like an international Test team, or a Barbarians select.

Tim Stimpson came in from West Hartlepool and was at full-back, Tony Underpants (Underwood) and Bentos (John Bentley) on the wings, Inga the Winga (Va'aiga Tuigamala) – who became the most expensive player in the world when he moved to Union from Wigan in the spring of 1997 – and Alan Tait, a Christmas present mid-season, were at centre, with Rob Andrew at number 10, Gazza at number 9.

Nick Popplewell, Ross Nesdale – a Kiwi who found someone in his family tree who liked Guinness or had an Irish Wolfhound, or who had an Irish Wolfhound that drank Guinness – was the hooker, and Georgie Porgie (George Graham) made up the front row. My unknown self was at lock, alongside Garath Archer who was an absolute beast, and was a trainer and a half – while I donated just a half – we were the boiler room and jumpers. Then the back row: Ten Bellies (Peter Walton), who got his nickname from Paul Gascoigne's pal Jimmy Five Bellies – except Walts really did have ten bellies, but was an absolutely unstoppable force; Pat Lam, Samoan, world-class, just magic in every area of back-row play, bolstered the pack mid-term; and Dean Ryan, England, beast, legend, nice guy occasionally, was at number 8 and captain, and coach. Mr Andrew was getting his money's worth there.

That was the main squad, but add into that mix the Gosforth guys I've mentioned, plus Andy Blyth, Graham Childs and Steve Douglas, and we had a proper team and squad, purposely manufactured for one thing – promotion and a place in the top flight. And I haven't even mentioned a young schoolboy by the name of Jonny Wilkinson.

Through time others would emerge: Jim Naylor, Jamie

Noon, Tom May, Ian Peel, John Leslie, Ross Beattie, Andrew Mower, Stuart Grimes, Micky Ward, Marius Hurter, Dave Walder, Hugh Vyvyan and several others. But everything that would emerge and grow at Newcastle came from the seeds planted by Rob Andrew in that first year after professionalism came in. Of course, Sir John Hall funded the seed buying.

I'd never say I was any kind of people watcher, or amateur psychologist, but how Rob Andrew bolted that team together I found fascinating, a real cross between social and sporting engineering. I would see it again a year later with the Lions, but I was intrigued to see how a team was formulated from so many diverse individuals.

The attitude of the professional players recruited from rugby league certainly pushed the standards in rugby union. Some of the things they did looked a bit strange and different. Then you realised they were doing it for a reason, that it was making them better players, that doing the drills and workouts made them faster, fitter, stronger, more explosive. Among those was Alan Tait, and Taity was a player. He was also the tightest man in the world, the sort who might have invented copper wire while fighting over a penny.

Alan was a Great Britain rugby league international and had reached the heights at club level with Widnes and Leeds. He was quite individualistic, quite a thinker about the game, and you could see that he'd worked out exactly how to play to his strengths. Defensively he was always there, seldom thereabouts. He seemed to have an uncanny ability to be in the right place. Then you realised that was because he was pushing, shepherding opponents into areas where they had no space to work. In attack, his lines and angles of running were such that he almost always appeared to take the ball at speed, and always exploited the weakest part of any defence, or his opposite number. Alan was a cracking player, who never felt guilty about leaving the party early, particularly when it was his shout.

He took a rugby league contract and embraced professionalism when that was a dirty word in our game, because it meant being paid to play and breaking your ties with the Union code. Not always liked, but in Alan's case, I think he was so focused on what he wanted to achieve that he didn't really give the condemnation or criticism too much of a second thought after leaving Kelso. And now, lo and behold, from being a mould-breaker in switching to League, he suddenly becomes the very type of player Union guys were themselves to be moulded into.

Taity and George Graham, another who had gone from Union to League, and now back again, were complete opposites, both in terms of their approach and, I imagine, their respective pay scales while playing League. But both were incredibly driven by the desire to be the best, and would do whatever it took to earn those prizes.

George was a different breed again to Alan, more of a fighter, usually with his shadow, aggressive beyond belief, like a bulldog that had lost its bone, then swallowed a wasp trying to find it. I looked at him a few times in matches and thanked Rob Andrew for signing him, because he'd have been a nightmare to play against.

George had come out of Stirling County, actually the

notorious Raploch scheme, which is probably why he fought so hard for everything in rugby. He was overlooked by Scotland and decided to earn a few quid by playing for Carlisle after his days in the army were over. That army connection was one reason why he and Dean Ryan got on well together. Like Gary Armstrong, the call from Newcastle, and the contract he was offered, meant George got the chance to earn something out of the game quite late in his career – he'd be in his thirties by the time he was first capped – but he still had a successful career for club and country.

Yes, he'd played for Carlisle. But he was earning a pittance compared to what he was on at the Falcons, and good luck to him. George isn't the biggest, an unfortunate disability as a rugby player. But because he was so low to the floor, he offered you something very special when scrummaging and he was a real grafter. His dedication was never in doubt. He travelled through from Carlisle, across the A69, every day, and even had his kids born in his home town of Stirling, although that might not necessarily have worked out the way he planned it.

My abiding memory of Georgie Porgie was with Scotland, in Dublin, at the old Lansdowne Road, when we lost heavily, but George managed to get a score. Unfortunately, in getting the ball down, he was injured. All I remember seeing was him being carried off.

Afterwards, we wanted to know what he'd done.

'I dislocated my shoulder,' he replied, still rather ashen-faced by the painful experience.

'So why were you carried off on a stretcher when your legs still worked?'

I don't think he was in the mood to joke about it. Of course, these days George is now better known as the 'father of Gary and Guy Graham', boys who followed their dad to the Falcons, although Gary has, internationally, committed himself to them on the other side of Hadrian's Wall. I'm saying nothing. I could have a similar debate in the future.

Taity and George showed the divergence, and the mixture, that Rob Andrew was formulating to make Newcastle an instant success. But of all of those names and recruits, the one that really put Newcastle on the map was Inga. He showed that Newcastle would buy the biggest and best to get the job done – and, at that point in time, that's exactly what Inga was.

One of the quietest, nicest individuals you could ever meet, he's a lovely human being away from rugby. On the pitch, however, he just tried to run through things, and occasionally over them: his opposite number, his pals, entire back rows. Land Rovers or houses wouldn't have been safe either. Inga wasn't all power and speed, although that helped and it's quite easy to focus on those strengths. He also had tremendous ball-handling skills, was a great support player in attack and defence, and had a good eye for an opening.

Maybe not the best trainer and, as an expert in that field I am, of course, able to pass comment. But all in, I think it was money well spent bringing Inga to Newcastle, and into the Union code.

In those early days, new faces were drip-fed into the squad. There were guys I was familiar with, but only in as much as I'd see them once, maybe twice a season on international duty, because they'd be playing in and for a different country. And now we were thrown together.

It was an interesting dynamic, but I think the general feeling was that we were all as one now, and shared a mutual respect that, even if you hadn't previously liked or fancied someone as a player, those on high – Rob Andrew, Steve Bates or Dean Ryan – had deemed them as capable or as useful as you in a certain position, so suck it up and get on with it. At Newcastle, because nearly everyone was or had been a new start at some stage, there wasn't the same 'us and them' mentality that some teams had to contend with.

There was a finding-out period when it came to new teammates. That would be the same with any new player at any club, pro or otherwise. So, you'd quickly see if some of the hype was true: was he immensely strong, or ultra quick, or phenomenally brave, or clever, or as they would have found out when they studied me, none of the above.

However, the main thing that changes the higher up the rugby ladder you go is the speed of the game and, it goes without saying, the reaction time and speed of thought among top players. To reach a certain level, you must have that. Taking that as a given, all you are looking for are the traits and nuances that make one player different from another: how do these guys work, what are their preferences at line-outs, are they two-footed, are they better going left or right? It doesn't sound much, but understanding these often minuscule features could mean the difference between winning and losing. You needed to be switched on.

It made training, dare I say it, a joy, because everyone

knew exactly how to apply the drills, set plays and moves, and the ball wasn't being dropped every two minutes.

At any given time there could have been four, even five players, all vying for two places, if you take my position at lock as an example. Whereas in the amateur game you might have had a couple of regulars and a couple in reserve, at Newcastle, as it would have been at other clubs, you suddenly had players being hired based on their ability, each of them thinking they were better than the other. Pride and egos could have got in the way. But, whether it was because of the management that was in place, or that we were all behaving like big boys who understood the script, I don't think we ever had any issues. Well, apart from where you got to sit in the changing room. Then there may have been a few prima donnas.

Ultimately, you had to play as one, and that also meant looking after each other, regardless of who you came up against, be that former teammates or current, fellow internationals.

But what a time we had that season when we got all the big weapons out the box, then added a few more along the way. We put seventy points on Nottingham, beat Blackheath by sixty-odd points, but drew with Richmond, our biggest rivals for the title and promotion, down at the Athletic Ground. Like Newcastle, Richmond had spent and recruited big: Ben Clarke, Brian Moore, Allan Bateman and the Quinnell brothers.

We were beginning to realise our full potential and, a few weeks into the season, Rugby were the unfortunate side that really copped it. When George Graham scored a hat-trick of tries, you knew something out of the ordinary had taken place. When Ross Nesdale does the same, you wince. The Falcons ran in twenty-four tries, and the score would have been even greater had Rob Andrew not missed half a dozen conversions. Final score 156–5. Impressive perhaps, but it highlighted the gulf between the clubs that would be there until the bigger, better resourced sides found their true level.

Then fourteen of us lost to Coventry. A defeat. This was unexpected. Bentos couldn't be held responsible as he wasn't on the field, red carded for punching someone. We lost twice that season, each time when we were reduced in numbers after a sending-off. The same thing happened at Bedford, Popps the guilty party that time, taking the law into his own hands after Scott Murray, my Scotland team-mate, had taken away my landing gear in a line-out. One thing we were good at was looking after one another.

However, those two losses – against good teams, it has to be said – put Richmond in the box seat and ultimately sent the title beyond our reach. But promotion, all along, had been the goal and we clinched that against Waterloo, so avoiding the play-offs, which ultimately did for Bedford and Coventry, Bristol and London Irish beating them respect-ively to preserve their Division One existence.

That season, though, we had really set the bar for the following campaign. We had scored 1,255 points in twenty-two games (you can work out the average), with John Bentley the top try-scorer with twenty-three, Gary Armstrong just behind on twenty-one.

We were in the big division and the expectations were big to match it. There can't have been many occasions when a team who have just won promotion (by finishing second, remember) were installed among the favourites for the Premier League title the next season, in among the establishment like Leicester, Bath, Saracens and Wasps. And Gloucester, Sale, Harlequins and Northampton. Nor should we forget Richmond, the team that pipped us for the second-tier crown.

An impressive list of rivals. However, there was no point in talking our chances down or bluffing that we were the new boys. People had seen what we were capable of. And so too had the Lions selectors, meaning that five of us boarded the plane to South Africa that summer.

One job done. A bigger task lay in wait.

15

Newcastle – Work, Rest and Play

NEWCASTLE AND LIFE AT THE FALCONS was a real special time for all involved. It was a fantastic place to be, because people never disconnected with the area. They were Geordies, immensely proud of it, and people who supported their own. It may have taken a wee while to earn acceptance, but once you had been adopted, as honorary Geordies, the support shown towards you was always generous.

People around Newcastle sort of knew who we were, eventually. But our profile was absolutely nothing like what the footballers enjoyed, or maybe that should be endured.

We got to know quite a few of them over the period, especially big Les Ferdinand – what a smashing guy – and the local boys like Steve Watson and Lee Clark in those early years, as well as Rob Lee and Shay Given – to a man, fantastic company with great craic. I can't say I knew Alan Shearer too well, even if we did share the same orthopaedic specialist.

Steve Black, our conditioning coach, fixer and occasional bodyguard, was a staunch Magpie, and he was in their camp. We would train at St James' Park occasionally, and the match staged there back in March 2018 against Northampton, when the Falcons wore the famous United stripes and the My Name'5 Doddie Foundation logo (when, ironically, a former United ball-boy Toby Flood kicked the winning points), gave us a chance to reminisce about the times we'd spent there, often running up and down the stands because the weather 'outside' during the winter was too poor. What a killer that was, and no hiding place. It had to be done, although you did have your pick of a seat if you needed a sit down.

We'd socialise with the footballers sometimes, finding ourselves invited to the same functions or race meetings, although keeping up with their expensive tastes could be damaging to the old credit card. Nick 'Popps' Popplewell recalls a great story of how we went out with them one night and every round of drinks was around four hundred quid. Each time it was our round, he says – by complete coincidence – we were at the toilet. We still went home full, though.

From my experience, I can't recall shouting a round too often either. The footballers were generous blokes. Maybe that was their lifestyle, how they relaxed. We might have thought we had it bad at times, but they couldn't cross the street without drawing attention to themselves. And the public adored them. I don't think I could live with that level of scrutiny; at times it must have been harder going out for a quiet meal than facing Manchester United or Arsenal.

There was no social media then, there wasn't even so much as a camera phone. So all you've really got today are memories, and they are wonderful. There are the odd photographs from functions, but selfies hadn't been invented. I look at things now, and five minutes after you've met someone and posed for a picture, it's up on Facebook or Twitter. I don't have a problem with that. That's where the world is now, and if you don't want your photograph to appear somewhere, don't pose for the photo. As I say, I don't have any issues with it. If anything, in the last year and a bit, it has been a brilliant form of media in maintaining and keeping my profile high for the work I'm doing.

But having seen the football players at close hand in the 1990s, I often wonder how utterly claustrophobic life must be for those guys today.

All I will say is that twenty years ago, thank goodness there weren't cameras on mobiles. It could have been very incriminating, for some. Not me. By 1997, I was an old married man, who lived outside Newcastle, so I could sneak home, unseen.

★

Professionalism had brought a new way of life, and especially a mix of different cultures. At the Falcons the best example of that was during the summer months when we'd still spend time together, but this was time for socialising and entertaining. And then the 'Island Boys' killed that stone dead. Let me explain.

Summer meant barbecues: charcoal fired up, who wants a

sausage, who wants a burger, a bit of chicken, a chop – oh, and a prawn. That's different. Then the islanders, Inga and Pat, had their date on the social calendar. And the barbecue circuit got very, very serious.

While we went to Sainsbury's or Tesco, they were gathering and sourcing all their island foods and vegetables from various specialist providers – potatoes, salads and things I didn't know existed. And instead of your everyday meat, they would have a couple of pigs or a boar impaled on a log, a fire pit dug in the ground, taking turn about at slowly rotating the carcass.

When we arrived, the expectation was to be met by the usual waft of firelighters, maybe even diesel and incinerated meat. Instead the smell was mouthwatering, and we'd be given slices or joints of this utterly succulent, juicy, irresistible meat. Barbecues would never quite be the same, and neither would some of our lawns. I mean, what could be difficult about cooking in an earth pit? Quite a lot as it transpired, which at least once led to an expensive disaster on the meat front, and what might best be described as a scorched grave in the lawn. The result of this failure? A hurried, desperate phone call for possibly the biggest order KFC in Newcastle ever had.

★

In those early days of professionalism, we had to sell the team, the concept and ourselves to the local community. It meant visiting a lot of schools, colleges and businesses around Newcastle to try and get people to buy into the

Falcons dream. Me and Marius Hurter, who is basically a South African version of the Incredible Hulk, made a pretty formidable sales team, if you like your salesmen of a freakish nature and likely to induce nightmares.

Me, I was never quite sure who we struck the most fear into during these visitations: the wee girl in P2 who thought some kind of giants had walked into her classroom, or the businessman who thought some kind of giants had walked in with more than a hint of menace to demand sponsorship.

At schools, we'd give impromptu geography lessons. All I had to do was point to a map, find Newcastle, and then run my finger up the coast and there was Scotland and where I used to live. In contrast, all Marius had to do was pull his finger down the map until he came to a big blue bit at the bottom and then stop at the last land mass, and that was South Africa. I must say, it regularly impressed the kids and, if truth be known, we regularly impressed ourselves.

Then, you didn't expect us to be trying to teach English, history or mathematics, did you?

We had a great mix within the dressing room, and there was always someone who could find, or procure, whatever someone else needed or required. Take Tony Underwood. Apart from having the most enthusiastic rugby supporter in the world in his mum, Annie, Tony also had excellent contacts with Land Rover. He drove a sponsored Range Rover and said they were looking for someone to pioneer and promote their new Discovery range. I thought, *Ah-ha, there's an opportunity. I'm game for that.* Country boy, huntin', shootin', fishin' sort, farmer. Right up their street.

Tony did the introductions and I did my bit, providing

appearances, doing some things with guests like clay pigeon shooting and off-roading around various country houses, estates and castles. I would also throw in the odd autographed ball or shirt, or come up with a couple of tickets for big games. It turned out to be a very worthwhile relationship.

I was delighted to help them and got a new car every six months. And a petrol card. Eventually I worked my way up to the top of the range. Those big V8s were thirsty. Hence why I had a petrol card.

In the end I kept my various wheels for about four years. Tony, however, only got to use his for a year, bless him. Maybe I enjoyed the corporate stuff more than he did!

But I never forgot Tony and what he did for me, all because I used to wave and ask what he was driving now. Actually, I could tell you exactly what he's driving right now – probably a long-haul flight out of the United Arab Emirates. I wonder if he gets a petrol card with that?

Tony was a bit like myself in that the Falcons project gave us a big stage to play on and that was a significant factor, I believe, in us getting selected for the Lions tour of South Africa in 1997.

Another who gave me some wheels, but only for a day, was Paul Mackings, who was CEO at the Falcons and one who liked his cars, a bit like myself. It's not all about John Deere tractors in life, you know.

Just after the World Cup in 1999, we'd been playing down in London, against Wasps at Loftus Road, and Gary injured his shoulder. Paul had driven down to the game, but such was the camaraderie within the entire Falcons set-up, even between senior executives at the club and the players, that he was another who enjoyed a game of cards and the banter on the bus – although I never did quite take as much money from him as I did from Sir John. But then, the big boss man never really got the Border tick-tack that was going on between me and Gazza.

This particular day, Paul asked if anyone wanted to drive his motor back up to Newcastle. I quite fancied getting up the road a bit quicker, and Gary wanted home as well because he was miserable and in pain with his shoulder dislocated. We stuck forty quid of petrol in the tank – it was a lot cheaper in them days than it is today – and away we went.

Coming up the M1 in this five-litre Mercedes, I was probably just enjoying the ride a bit too much, because next thing the blue lights and sirens are behind us, so I pull in and jump out, just to show the police officers that I was really keen to meet them. And they were so pleased to see me, they offered me a seat in the back. Friends already.

'And what's your name?'

'Doddie Weir.'

'Doddie Weir? The rugby player Doddie Weir?'

I nodded. Maybe I had a rugby fan.

'I had ten quid on you to win the World Cup.'

I didn't feel confident at that point and had ditched the idea of him even knowing anything about the game, never mind being a fan.

'I'll tell you what,' I said, quick as a flash. 'I'll give you your tenner back right now and I'll be on my way.'

'You can't say that. This conversation is being recorded.'

'Well, I'll get out and I'll ask you again.'

'Stop, no, enough.'

He asked where I'd been and what I was doing, so I explained that Gary was actually in the car, injured, and not too happy as he was in need of some more painkillers. The police driver went to have a look, just to confirm, and there was wee Gazza, with the big long face, arm in a sling, looking at him from the back seat.

'We made it ninety-four.'

'I'm really sorry, officer,' I said, thinking, *Phew, at least it wasn't a ton.*

'Well, it's your lucky day, because we've just had a call and need to go. Get yourself away and ease up.'

'Yes, officer. Thank you, officer.'

And, with that, I jumped out and back into the Mercedes. I was working out how to start this flying machine again, and there was a chap at the window. My friendly policeman.

'It's not your lucky day after all. The shout has been cancelled. Just get in the back again.'

Seriously, I know he'd lost a tenner but that was a bit extreme. And that was the last time I did Armstrong any favours.

16

Nearly, Nearly, Finally

Going into 1995, there was nothing to suggest that a few months later we'd be tripping on down to London for another Grand Slam decider.

1994, and I had been part of it, was at best a write-off results-wise for Scotland. We lost in Cardiff, lost to the last kick of the game at Murrayfield against England, drew 6–6 with Ireland in Dublin and lost to France at home, so ended up comfortably claiming the Wooden Spoon.

Quite a few of us opted not to tour Argentina that summer, a trip that resulted in two losses against the Pumas, before the South Africans rounded off a miserable year at Murrayfield, a match which put my Scotland career in the balance.

A pointer that the new year might offer something better came against Italy in an 'A' international at McDiarmid Park in Perth, early January 1995. The Italian performance that day put a few in the frame for an international against Canada two weeks later. Remember, this was in the days of the Five Nations, so every country effectively had a free week at some stage, and the game against Canada brought everyone up to speed ahead of the main event.

Dave Hilton made his debut, but of more interest to me was Stewart Campbell being picked at lock, and Eric Peters at number 8. That meant no place in the team for me, and similarly when we played and beat Ireland with a bit of style, although I was on the bench then.

Next match was away to France. We hadn't won over there since 1969 when a certain Jim Telfer scored the winning try – so long ago that the footage was in black and white. And we had never won in the Parc des Princes. More chance of leaving there black and blue.

But, against the odds, we won 23–21 and I even made it back onto the pitch. Damian Cronin sustained elbow ligament damage, so I was called on at half time. The French outscored us in the match 3–2 on tries, but they missed all their conversions, unlike Gavin Hastings, who after his lung-bursting break for the line to score under the posts had to get up, compose himself, and hit the conversion for the win. Not that I appeared too interested in that minor detail, sauntering back to halfway.

While Gav finished it off, it was the genius of Gregor Townsend that created it. Around this time in rugby, we were hearing a lot about rugby league influences creeping into the game, particularly in the off-load area. But Toony's back of the hand flick to his captain owed much more to Sevens rugby than St Helens or Salford. Watch it today; it is still a wonderful piece of skill.

Having not won in Paris for twenty-six years, there was a bit of lost time to be made up for that night. What a celebration we had. The hotel we were in was full of couches, big armchairs and chaise longues on every floor. So, we thought we'd have a tidy up and redistribute them more evenly, all up to the corridor on the very top floor.

The wee manager just smiled as his furniture disappeared to on high. I think his smile was painted on, as he just kept looking at the running total on the bar tab, which was accelerating to a new SRU record. But who cared. I think Damian forgot about his elbow being painful, helped by some pure malt pain relief, although Ian Jardine needed something a bit stronger having had his cheekbone fractured. It took away some of his good looks.

We were two out of two, and from a completely selfish position, I had got back in the team, at lock. But no one was getting too far ahead of themselves despite the one hundred per cent record, probably because even though we were at home, we expected a response from a Wales team that had lost badly to France and England.

Again, versus Wales, we turned in an excellent performance, capped off by one of the great Scotland tries, scored by Eric Peters, who was utterly outstanding that season. There was much made of this relatively unknown ex-English Under-21s and Students cap (although he was born in Glasgow) making it this far with Scotland. But, simply put, Eric played for Bath and, truthfully, given who they had in terms of Ben Clarke, Steve Ojomoh, Andy Robinson, John Hall and before that Dave Egerton, it was probably harder to get in the Bath XV than it was the Scotland team. I mean, we were hardly blessed with good number 8s . . .

And, with that, suddenly we were into another Five

Nations Championship, Grand Slam, Triple Crown and Calcutta Cup decider at Twickenham. I've never been one for getting cranked up or bothered ahead of matches. I can't therefore say I was overly excited or made nervous by the prospect. What I do recall was that spirits within the camp were great, very jovial, more positivity than pessimism.

England were a very good team, with a pretty good pack of forwards who had the ability to grind and wear you down. Craig Chalmers thought they were slow, especially when coming off the back of scrums or rucks on opposition ball. Chick, being Chick, and never one not to back himself, thought three drop goals were well within his sights. He actually got two.

The English pack had turned the rolling maul into a snooze-inducing art form, extremely effective and very hard to halt. Not attractive, but effective. We, however, thought we had schemed a way of at least disrupting it enough to make it less effective. And it worked, up to a point, the point being Irish referee Brian Stirling – or Brian Surrey as one wag christened him – who just did not see it our way. I can still hear his whistle today. Which meant that Rob Andrew kicked us to death, with seven penalties and a drop goal in a 24–12 win. Job done for England, but a game easily forgotten about from our perspective.

Brian Moore, wee Mr Angry himself, sounded off, accusing us of 'killing the ball and the game at all costs' or some such. That wasn't true. Peter Wright had also tried to kill Will Carling. To be fair – and he always was – Carling and coach Jack Rowell didn't agree with their hooker.

Brian, nicknamed 'The Pitbull', riled me so much that in my newspaper column I said he should be put down. Ach, I was emotional.

I'm glad, however, that he wasn't. He would eventually come in handy later in life, as will become apparent.

After the usual dinner, it was all back to the Gloucester Road hotel. We'd lost, but we had performed better than expected, and there was a World Cup to look ahead to. A small beer was perfectly in order.

What was unexpected was that three or four of the England team arrived back with us, confident that our wake would be much better than the English celebrations. How could we refuse them?

In the wee small hours, a piano suddenly emerged in the hotel bar we had invaded. Not more furniture removals after our Paris exploits, I thought. No, it was for someone to play. I've always found the best way of doing these things is to find someone who can play a piano first, rather than deliver one on the off chance there might be a budding Jools Holland among us.

Fortunately there was. Former Scotland hooker and selector Colin Fisher rattled the old ivories. I wasn't really listening, but he appeared to give us more than 'Chopsticks' or 'Three Blind Mice'.

Kenny Logan went missing. It was easy to tell as the decibel level had gone down a few notches in his absence. He returned an hour later, looking cold.

'Where were you?'

'The toilet.'

'You were away a while?'

'I fell asleep in the gents with the window open. I'm frozen.'

'Do you want something to warm you up?'

'Please.'

'Right, get the next round in. That'll get your blood temperature up.'

There wasn't any soul searching that night, or wildly optimistic expectations being made for the World Cup, or for the next Five Nations in twelve months. Being Scottish, you just don't do that. Therefore, when the 1996 Championship came about, even matching the current season's success would be a tall order (no pun intended).

Rob Wainwright had inherited the captaincy after Gavin Hastings retired, with Rowen Shepherd taking the full-back berth. But he wasn't a natural replacement as a kicker, so, to fix that problem, Michael Dods, ex of Gala and now of Northampton, was accommodated on the wing. Would it work?

16–3 up at half time in Dublin, with a try and a penalty from Dods, and another try from Kevin McKenzie, now first-choice hooker after Kenny Milne's retirement, suggested that there hadn't been too much upheaval. While Ireland came back, we held out with a good defensive effort in the second half. Meanwhile in Paris, England lost. No Grand Slam this season for the defending champions.

Remember those concerns about 'Peapod' (don't ask) Dods? In not too dissimilar fashion to his big brother Peter twelve years earlier, the latterday Dodsy was playing a key role for Scotland. Two tries and three penalties made him our Man of the Match and game clincher as we toppled the French 19–14.

A fortnight on, and we squeezed Wales out 16–14 in Cardiff, Dods kicking eleven points, Toony coming good with a second-half try.

Referee Joel Dume wasn't best pleased when we decided to have a quick verse of 'Flower of Scotland' in our pre-kick-off huddle, singing away to ourselves as Cardiff Arms Park erupted in anticipation. That steeled us for the day, and we needed it.

Dodsy Mark II was in the thick of it. We conceded a penalty, well within range, and at a crucial point in proceedings, but John Davies had used Michael as a doormat and the award was reversed. It was a break we needed, and actually deserved.

16–9 up, in the closing seconds, Wales scored a try in the corner. Arwel Thomas, their young stand-off, kicked, but thankfully he pulled it and we had won.

Suddenly and unexpectedly, we were faced with the prospect of playing England to win the Grand Slam, while the English still had ambitions of a Triple Crown. There was merriment, mirth – much of it from Kenny Logan, who finally got on as a replacement for Craig Joiner, and whose break set up the scrum that Gregor Townsend's try came from – and no small measure of bemusement that we were, for a second year, eighty minutes away from completing only the fourth Grand Slam in Scotland's history.

The Welsh boys – captain Jonathan Humphreys, Ieuan Evans, Rob Howley – were gutted, but generous in their praise of how we'd won the game.

Our coach Richie Dixon, however, wasn't happy at our

efforts, saying that the best part of our game was defence, and that he couldn't 'give Wales enough credit'. Eh?

During a career of hearing the 180-degree logic and negative psychology of Jim Telfer, this was on a different plane to anything the now national coaching director had ever spun. We had beaten Wales, hadn't we?

The next fortnight would drag on, partly because I was still getting all the final details of my switch to Newcastle ironed out. It took months to eventually sort. Still, there were worse positions to be in as an international rugby player.

But ahead of another England derby, did we talk things up, talk them down, keep a lid on it, or rattle a few cages? What we did know, without anyone really spelling it out, was that being at home, at Murrayfield, rather than at Twickenham, gave us an even better chance than last year.

The giveaway to what kind of English team we would be taking on came when they announced Dean Richards would be back at number 8. It was going to be forward-orientated, with England playing 'up the jumper' rugby, again.

And guess what. England won 18–9 in a try-less kicking competition where we gave them – and Paul Grayson – more chances by conceding more penalties and territory. It was quite dispiriting really, and another disappointment because we had allowed England to dictate again.

And with that, another chance for major honours and silverware had gone. By nature, I have been optimistic rather than pessimistic, half full – literally on occasions – rather than half empty. However, you do wonder, when opportunities have passed, especially with Scotland, and when you are constantly coming up against the might of England, if you'll ever get another.

★

The years 1997 and 1998 saw us win two matches, both against Ireland, consigning them to the Wooden Spoon. Then in November 1997, Christmas arrived early. Actually, Santa delivered Glenn Metcalfe and Gordon Simpson as new caps in Australia. For the Autumn Test against South Africa, John and Martin Leslie, Jamie Mayer and Anthony Charles 'Budge' Pountney debuted. Of that sextet, only Mayer was Scots-born. By now, we were actively pushing the envelope when it came to recruitment.

They were all in the frame for the first game of the last Five Nations the following January, against Wales. Sadly Mayer and Simpson had succumbed to injury by then, as had captain Bryan Redpath, an ankle injury ruling him out for the entirety of the tournament. Deputising, both at scrum-half and as captain, would be Gary Armstrong.

If anyone wanted to know what qualities John Leslie brought to the team, you only had to wait nine and a half seconds into the Welsh game to find out. Duncan Hodge took the kick-off and went to the blindside, where Leslie caught the ball and sprinted over for the score. We won 33–20, but my contribution to the entire campaign lasted forty-four minutes.

In first-half stoppage time, I won a line-out off Gordon Bulloch's throw inside our own 22. However, I landed awkwardly and was left to limp off with the physios at the interval. After examination, an X-ray later confirmed that I'd broken my ankle. And that was it for me, other than trying to explain to Rob Andrew when I got back to Newcastle.

Scotland, who incredibly had a Captain Carling piloting their flight to Heathrow, lost to England at Twickers, albeit one of the more attractive matches to watch, then beat Ireland and France, the latter – a 36–22 win in Paris – being one of our greatest performances ever. And that was the season over.

England would play on the Sunday at Wembley. All they had to do was beat Wales to lift yet another Grand Slam. But my old Lions mate Scott Gibbs had other ideas, hitting the line on a crash ball, bursting through the English cover to skip and dance over for a try. Another from that South African adventure, Neil Jenkins, kicked the winning conversion and Wales celebrated a dramatic 32–31 victory. But they weren't alone in celebrating.

North of the border, that England loss meant we were crowned Five Nations Championship winners, and there-fore – unless something really untoward happens – the holders and undefeated champions for evermore.

Naturally, there had to be a presentation of the trophy, which took place at Murrayfield on the Monday night, a low-key affair compared to what it could have been. We had our pictures taken, one with me, Gazza and Walts posing, the Newcastle contingent who did so much for the Scotland cause. Where exactly Stuart Grimes, Alan Tait and John Leslie were at the time, who knows.

Gary is all blazered up, looking like the MD of a security

business. Peter and me look like hired heavies, guarding the trophy. We must have been good at it. The SRU still have it.

But that part was actually irrelevant. What mattered was that we had our first title since 1990, and I had been there. Okay, I had been there for one-eighth of it, but it still counts on my CV.

And next year, in 2019, we arrive at twenty years since our Five Nations success. Should be worth a reunion dinner at least.

17

Scotland

THERE ARE STOCK QUESTIONS you are asked whenever you do a rugby forum, or sit on a sponsors' panel. 'What's it like to play for Scotland?' has to be the most frequent, and for stock questions, there are some stock answers.

You talk about the pride, you say that it was always an honour, tell them what it was like to run onto the pitch at a packed Murrayfield and feel your chest swell with pride as the pipes and drums started to play 'Flower of Scotland'. And you talk about the support you receive, both on the day and from the nation as a whole. And that answer is entirely true.

However, there was always a part of me that looked upon being in the Scotland set-up as getting back out with my pals. Imagine, thirty of you all on a boys – or girls – long weekend, all paid for, where you can have an absolute hoolie.

Or, at the end of every season, if you'd done your job to the best of your ability, you all got taken on holiday for three or four or five weeks, to the other side of the world, on what in the industry was called 'a tour'.

Those were the real highlights for me about playing with Scotland. Yes, winning was great, but you weren't always guaranteed that. What you were certain of was that you'd pair up, or team up, with two dozen like-minded individuals. And let the party begin.

I should confess that throughout my career, rugby was all very sociable. You played, you could have a beer. No one went overboard. It was all quite measured, usually in pints. We were big boys, with big responsibilities, and we could be trusted. I think it's different today. Everyone appears to be watching over their shoulder. Is that why kids start playing rugby? I always thought it was for the fun of it.

If we were away with Scotland on tour, or on a trip back from a match, we'd have a couple of beers on the plane, what we called the Row 19 club. Because everything was done alphabetically, a great many times I'd find myself among my fellow 'Ws', which meant, being a Weir, I'd be in the company of Messrs Walton and Wainwright, and Peter Wright and Ian Smith (not a 'W') may have had the misfortune of having a membership as well.

I say a few beers, but actually we had a wee whisky, or two, especially if it was at the SRU's expense. And it would be good stuff, as Wainwright was quite well educated that way, a bit of a connoisseur, and would always ask what whiskies were on the menu before ordering on our behalf. Very cultured, although lost much of the time on me and Walts.

Peter Walton is a good guy, but let's be honest, he isn't even Scottish. He won twenty-odd caps based on his good attendance at Merchiston. His mum was a great home baker, though. You only need to look at Walts to appreciate that. But he is a fine specimen with a wonderful family and, as I saw with Scotland and Newcastle, a total juggernaut when he got going. He could just bump people off while running and, staying low to the turf at the same time, was very difficult to stop. If you wanted someone to punch holes in the opposition defence, especially on short-yardage plays, Walts was an effective weapon.

By contrast, Wainwright is one of those guys you don't want to like. There is nothing he can't do. He's good looking, quite suave, well spoken, went to Cambridge where he won a blue at rugby – and boxing, as you do – qualified as a doctor, was a Major in the army, and once used to keep a buzzard as a pet. And he can sing and dance.

We almost became teammates at West Hartlepool when their owner, Phillip Yuill, put me on his car insurance – so I could drive his Ferrari.

Now Rob lives on the island of Coll, has his own beach and catches his dinner daily – lobster, crab or whatever fish swims past – and gets his honey from his own hives.

Wainwright was always quite handy with a rod. Before we went to South Africa for the World Cup in 1995, Famous Grouse put on some activity days for us. This included golf at St Andrews, where Dave Hilton took the course apart, quite literally, then blamed it on the 'sticks'; while in a driving competition, Cammy Glasgow barrel-rolled a Honda Pilot buggy down this massively steep hill. We were frightened to look over the edge in case there was no more Cammy.

We also had a fly-fishing competition, where you had to

hit ten cones, five in a line and five at forty-five degrees, so you had to keep lengthening the line. People were catching teammates, whipping players with the rod, even throwing the rod away. Wainwright, though, got full points, then won the clay pigeon shooting for good measure.

He should have auditioned for the role of James Bond at some point in his life – and, for all the reasons and examples listed, this is why I'd really like not to like him. That and the fact that women all love him. He is, granted, fantastic company and also very funny (I should have added those items to my list), as I've seen when he has done some of the corporate stuff at Murrayfield.

A few years ago, he turned up for one of the Six Nations matches with pink hair. Now, he was approaching fifty at that point, and I wondered if he was going through some kind of midlife crisis, or maybe was trying to tell us something. I had to ask.

It transpired that on Boxing Day they'd staged a big event in aid of a cancer charity, and his kids had convinced him to dye his hair pink and assured him it would wash out the next day. The match Rob turned up for at Murrayfield was in February.

But he just laughed it off, having done his bit for charity, and he's still doing it, having been a wonderful supporter of me and the Foundation and what I've been trying to do since my diagnosis. His Doddie Gump idea was just genius.

Last year, on my Islands of the World tour, we visited Wainwright on Coll and attended the local agricultural show, along with Mary Doll and the 'Double Gloucester' boys Ian Smith and Pete Jones and twenty loaves of bread.

Why all the bread? Because I had misread the text and was eighteen over. He'd only asked for two!

An agricultural show isn't the same unless you are competing, so after farmer Wainwright selected the best of his flock, we selected the best of the leftovers – and made a clean sweep of the prizes.

Back in the day, Rob was one of the Thursday Club members. Thursday was when we gathered at Murrayfield ahead of international matches, which was then changed to a Wednesday, just for the forwards because we were special and carried the rest of the team. That meant we got out on the town for a night, just for a shandy – or quite a lot of beers, if truth be told. It was all part of the adventure, a wee bonus for having been picked in the first place, and you were always going to run it out your system again on the Thursday. And then one or two of the backs got to hear about our extra preparations and decided that it might be no bad thing if they joined in as well, and they were made more than welcome. Some were impressed by our levels of dedication. If only they knew. Actually, I think they did.

I have no doubt there will be dieticians and performance coaches reading this and drawing up a list of the pitfalls and drawbacks of doing that in the week leading up to a game. But I, at no time, thought it damaging. If anything, I think it brought us even closer together. I've witnessed it from the other side, and I know what I prefer, and what I think brings out the best in people.

And win or lose, we would have just one almighty mad session after the game on the Saturday, whether in Edinburgh, or Dublin, or wherever, where we got to chill, and to meet some of the boys we'd knocked the shit out of that afternoon. There were some truly bonkers nights after Five Nations matches: presidents' receptions, out to a few bars, back to the hotel for a night cap with your breakfast, all slept off the next day.

There was the night in Paris when one of the motorcycle cops and I hit it off, and he took me for a spin on the back of his motorbike. I was quite drunk, and didn't have a helmet on as we sped through Paris, me holding on for dear life with one arm, and trying desperately to stop my kilt from blowing up and over my head, unsuccessfully I should add, which had drivers honking their horns. Then we stopped. He was lost.

But you could do that then. A bit like racing golf carts at Dalmahoy with Graham Shiel. No mobiles, no cameras, back when Twitter was something birds did. Imagine that now.

Today, teams choose to jet home after games. Different times, different disciplines. I get that and take my hat off to them for being so disciplined. But, you put a lot into being an international rugby player, and I'd want to get a little bit back out. I think today's professional is missing that side of the game.

There are people who have almost total recall, who possess a forensic-like memory and have logged every single airport, squad, hotel, result, type of bus or plane and what weather we'd experienced. Writing this book, I have to declare, I do not fall into that category. Is that because I've had a bang on the head at some time? I don't know, I can't remember that either.

Seriously, I think some of it is because you are so caught up in the moment, in the experience, that you don't really have time to think about what is happening. I do wish that I had made more of the occasions and events in and around my career, like World Cups, cup finals and the likes. People say enjoy the moment, but I honestly think I was so caught up in the here and now that I never really thought about anything other than what was going to happen in the dressing room, or on the field. It is sad in a way, especially when others talk about things and appear to have enjoyed them more than you – although I know that isn't true. I loved every moment I was involved.

But so much of sport is about one season merging into a summer tour, which then runs into the next season. You do remember the bigger, more significant events – or in my case, the more bizarre and outrageous occurrences.

For instance, in 1996, the summer tour was to New Zealand, memorable because it was New Zealand, and because Gary – now that he was getting paid for a living – had decided to play international rugby again.

In the First Test, we scored three tries but unfortunately the All Blacks scored five between them, and Christian Cullen scored another four of his own for good measure as we were hammered 63–31.

However, many experts and coaches will tell you that you should always take something out of a defeat. From that one, I took that Ronnie Eriksson, who made his debut at centre, appeared in the programme as 'BRS Eriksson' and subsequently found out that his real first name was actually Bo. Who knew?

Amazing that you play for your country, against the All Blacks, and that is all you take from the match.

We also lost the Second Test. However, the thing that still sticks in the memory from that trip was our hotel in Wanganui catching fire. As we waited for what seemed an age to be allowed back in to the hotel, Rob Wainwright, the captain on that tour, suddenly emerged with a towel over his arm and declared, 'Right, f*** this, I'm going for a bath.'

That was also the trip where I managed to sleep through an earthquake. Actually, I did hear something, but thought it was Peter Wright, snoring at the other end of the hotel.

On that tour Scott Hastings – who I'd liked ever since he made 'that' tackle on Rory Underwood at Murrayfield in 1990 – was entrusted with the key role of social convenor. I say 'key', because when you are on tour, and you have some down time, you want to make the most of it. Who better then to be given that position of authority than a Grand Slam winner and a Lions tourist, no less.

The bold Scott decided that maybe we needed a little pick-me-up mid trip, so he organised a dancer to come and entertain the troops. Having been away from the wives and girlfriends for a good few weeks, this was an entirely appropriate morale-booster, team-bonder and social highlight of the week, maybe the entire year given how delighted Scott was with his capture.

The assembled audience were poised in anticipation, with much strategic placing of seats and chairs for the best possible vantage point as the music began and the lights went down – then came back up again to reveal . . . a bloke on the stage.

Scott would have you believe he did it for a laugh. Knowing Scott, I don't think he's that clever. No matter, it was just so incredibly funny, almost as much as the party was incredibly good.

Having Gary back on that New Zealand trip meant there was now the possibility of the gruesome twosome – Armstrong and Redpath – getting back in tow in the future.

They were terrible. On the pitch, game time, few better in my mind. Take them off the training ground, or out of the weights room, whenever they had down time, they had the capability to create hell and no one was safe.

Gary's stock jokes at the dinner table involved salt on people's meals when they weren't watching, or dampening the cutlery and sticking salt on the bottom side of spoons and forks. I'm sure some of the time he didn't use a glass of water and just licked them. But it was such a childish prank, and there wasn't anyone he didn't catch out, sometimes on every course of a meal.

They'd also break into your room, cover the handset of the phone in the room with Vaseline, then ring it. When you answered, if you hadn't dropped the receiver, all you would hear would be the two of them giggling like daft schoolboys.

And then there was the time at Dalmahoy, Edinburgh, when JJ was settling down to watch TV and the channel kept changing, so he'd change it back. Eventually he called the manager, who gave him a new remote control. Working perfectly, he sat down again, but then the same thing happened, channels skipping themselves and JJ becoming extremely frustrated.

If it hadn't been for Gary and me – he was on my shoulders and armed with a remote control – laughing outside his bedroom window, we'd have got away with it.

Jim Telfer would tell you himself that Gazza and Brush tormented the living daylights out of him, not because he was the target or victim, but as Jim would say, 'I know some other poor bugger is suffering because of that pair.'

Jim was big into us going for walks, getting a bit of air, a bit of a stretch, and the chance to talk or just relax before or after the next session. But Gary and Bryan would see this as an opportunity, away from prying eyes.

They'd come back, having found a felled tree, with their pockets full. Next thing you'd know, someone had bitten into their cheese sandwich and found it full of sawdust. Of course, Gary and Bryan had scurried away to leave someone else to take the blame.

Or they'd collect dock leaves and fire them in to some unsuspecting teammate's salad. Seeing someone munch their salad and watching as they reached the part that tasted different was very funny.

Rugby players of my generation are not, in general, fussy eaters. You ate what you liked, and more of the same if you really liked it. Along the way, the dieticians came into play, with their shakes, drinks, and lists of what to eat and when to eat it. All that happened for me was that in trying to produce leaner, meaner, hungrier players, you ended up with meaner, angrier players simply because they were hungry.

Eric Peters was the strangest, in as much as he'd bring his own food to cook on a Friday night. As I said, the dieticians were advising us what and when we should eat, we had fitness experts, we had access to brilliant chefs, as you would do in some of the hotels where we stayed, but when we were at Dalmahoy, or away in Ireland or France, wherever, Ecky the Dunt would disappear down to the kitchen to cook his pasta. I don't know if it was special pasta, or a fancy recipe, or fancy shapes, or Alphabetti Spaghetti. He never gave me a taste. I haven't seen him on telly rivalling Gordon Ramsay, so maybe that was the only thing he could cook. Very peculiar but, hey, each to their own.

Eric, who came through his own trials and tribulations along the way, was a cracking player and a lovely guy, and scored one of the all-time great Scotland tries against Wales in 1995, although he never thanked me for making a wonderful break halfway through the move from our own 22 that set up the try – and Kenny Logan may have contributed something along the way, I can't remember.

Because of all the squads you were involved in, all the matches, the trips and the tours, you never forget what it meant to be part of the Scotland set-up, or what it meant to be a Scotland player. It is something that never leaves you.

And in November 2017, the SRU gave me a moment that will never leave me, namely walking out onto the pitch at Murrayfield ahead of the New Zealand game.

The Scottish Rugby Union were great, as they have been all through this chapter of my life, and they could not have been more helpful or supportive. They went above and beyond, even breaking broadcast rules with the hashtag logo on the pitch. I think they got away with it . . .

Being guest of honour and walking out on to the Murrayfield pitch ahead of the New Zealand match was such a privilege. On the Friday, we had the final run through on what would happen. I'd have the ball, I walk to the fifteen-metre line with Hamish, Angus and Ben, where they would stop, and I'd leave them and continue out to the middle. I'd leave them. I tell myself not to think that way, it's just a turn of phrase, but it had been planted.

Then all I'd do is continue to walk, greet the captains, hand the ball to the referee. Job done.

Come game time, I'd played it out so often in my head, and discussed it with a few people, that I had now become comfortable with the idea. The boys seemed happy enough, just keep smiling, laughing, and it would soon be over. Then wham.

We were waiting at the back of the tunnel, ready to walk out and I was blindsided by Scotland coach Gregor Townsend, who gave me a big hug, the kind you get from guys you've tried to rattle because they were good, played against, played with, toured with, lost with and won alongside, the kind of embrace that doesn't need to be accompanied by any words. I said thanks. What I really wanted to say was, 'Oh, Toony, why did you have to do that?'

I tried to compose myself and go through the next play – walk, wave, then all I had to do was present the ball. Easy. Walk, wave and present the ball. What would be difficult in that? All I had to do was present the ball – like I did, on a plate, so often for Armstrong, Redpath, Nicol.

Walk, wave, present.

We started walking, and waving, but the lights from mobile phones flashing all just merged behind the tears. The boys reached their mark: 'I'll see you in a minute, boys.' My wingmen stopped and I was on my own. *Hold it together, big man.* I couldn't see much, but I could hear the crowd, I could feel my lip tremble.

I was greeted by Kieran Read, the All Blacks captain, and John Barclay, his opposite number with Scotland, who I'd been able to speak with in the week leading up to the game. Their words were welcome and touching. So were those of Beauden Barrett: 'Can I have the ball please, mate, so I can kick off?' Now, that did raise a smile. Fine having all these pleasantries, but here was a guy with a Test to win.

Turning around to come back off, however, was even more emotional. A few seconds before, I'd still been running to a script I'd thought through in my mind several dozen times, but I had never anticipated what it would be like heading in the opposite direction, when the anticipation of the crowd, ready for kick-off, was mixed with the farewell I was now receiving. Oh, that was hard. But at least the boys and the tunnel beckoned. And then I could relax, or at least get back to a state of calmness, ready to do my hospitality work upstairs.

And, for that, I won the prestigious Laureus Sporting Moment of the Month award.

Being at Murrayfield for that Autumn Test marked twenty-seven years from when, as a gangly young pup, I strode on to the field to face Argentina and make my Scotland debut.

A real adventure along the way, where the downs made the ups all the sweeter, and one which I would recommend to anyone.

18

The Millennium Falcon
Flies No More

THE 2000 SIX NATIONS STARTED badly and never got any
better. We were defending champions, having won the
final Five Nations tournament the previous spring. Actually,
we still are Five Nations champions, undefeated. I should
have used that line more over the years, so I'm making up
for that here!

The first game up would be in Rome, against the nation
which had taken the tournament from a five to six, and
that was Italy. Over a great many years, the Italians had
progressed through B then A internationals and on to full
Test status. Remember, they'd been playing in World Cups
as long as Scotland had.

The first time I'd played them in a full international was
in 1996, then again two years later when we lost in Treviso.
Italy had the capacity, in any game, to play like complete
novices – they had conceded a century of points against the
All Blacks in the previous year's World Cup – or throw the
ball around like the Barbarians and match any team in the

world up front. They also had a world-class kicker in Diego Dominguez, as Scotland had seen in 1998.

'In Dominguez, at stand-off, Italy do have a class player,' I said, with stupid, visionary confidence, in the *Mirror* on the morning of the game.

'He is very good at directing play and is a fine kicker, from hand and in front of the posts. If there is one player we need to keep tabs on it's him.

'I saw him play for Stade Français in a European Cup tie and he was superb. And I'm not basing that on one game. Because the French don't tend to import or hire duds.'

I said all of that.

Maybe I should have done the astrology and horoscopes as well that day in the paper. Italy won 34–20.

It may have been the Italians' debut at this level, but they played it like it was a World Cup final. The Stadio Flaminio wasn't a big ground, but it was imposing, filled with fanatical fans. After the Italian national anthem had been played, several of the Azzurri pack were in tears. So were we by the end.

We lost John Leslie, our new captain and my Falcons teammate, after ten minutes to injury. Kenny Logan missed a couple of kicks (he did pay me not to say it was four or five), but up front we were mauled and bullied by the Italian pack, who played like men possessed.

Eventually they drove over for a try, with all eight forwards, 29,000 supporters, and every other rugby fan in Italy pushing and willing them over the line as one. Dominguez kicked the conversion to take his personal tally to twenty-nine points, which included three drop goals. Well, I had warned everyone about him!

That night – with the match ball already packed in my kit bag as a memento – was not one for sitting around a hotel, moping and crying into your beer. We could do that elsewhere, but where? Consult page 97 of the unofficial international rugby players' guide and search under 'How do you find out where to go in a strange city?' Answer – ask a polis on a motorbike. It worked everywhere else, why not Rome?

We weren't alone in drowning our sorrows, bumping into loads of Scotland fans doing the same thing, many hitting the town with wives and girlfriends. Couples on a rugby trip?

It appeared that in working out the new fixture list, which stretched the tournament to a full two months, the Six Nations computer had inadvertently tied Rome in with Cardiff and Dublin – the traditional destinations for away weekends. There appeared to be a trade-off taking place with fellas whisking their better half away for a romantic, rugby-themed weekend, so buying themselves Brownie points to make similar trips around the Celtic capitals, unaccompanied. It's something else Scotland gave the sporting world and, happily, a tradition (or maybe a necessity) that continues to this day, as we saw with the Doddie Gump March in 2018.

A fortnight after the failed Italian Job, we were off to Dublin. I started on the bench, being shaken violently by every DART train that passed under the main stand. Scotland were equally shaken up, losing 44–22. Another sore one, only eased – from what I remember – by developing a taste for Highland Park whisky in the company of Budge Pountney and Glenn Metcalfe later that night.

I was in from the off for the France game. We lost, as we did in Cardiff, the Welsh putting the infamous 'Grannygate' eligibility scandal – when Kiwis Shane Howarth and Brett Sinkinson were banned, having previously played for Wales, after discovering that grandparents hadn't been born where they'd originally thought – behind them to win. I was dropped to the bench and stayed there, unused against Wales. That night, we took over a bar in the city centre. No, we really took it over: Cammy Mather and Martin Leslie serving behind the bar, dishing out drinks like nobody's business. They were good at their job.

Sorry, they were good at fifty per cent of their job.

I'm surprised the pub didn't go out of business, as the pair of them were dishing up the booze, but weren't taking any money, just pouring pints and opening bottles. For once the flight from Cardiff to Edinburgh on the Sunday felt quite sombre. Maybe it was all the free drink.

That left us with one game to be played, against title favourites and Grand Slam-chasing England, but I was dropped, setting off a chain of events that for evermore has topped my irony of ironies list.

Firstly, Richard Metcalfe was selected to win his first cap, all seven foot of him. He had previously been selected for England A, but was eligible for Scotland through his granny, who was from Paisley. He would have probably still been hanging out for an England call at full international level had it not been for a couple of Scots – namely me and Alan Tait – 'tapping him up' while he was at Newcastle, suggesting he should look into his history to see if his family tree had any Scottish branches.

My last appearance in a Scotland shirt, against Joost van der Westhuizen and the Barbarians.

Playing Sevens for Scotland in the 'butcher's apron' jersey.

Winning a line-out against the All Blacks at the 1999 World Cup.

Having a heated debate with Neil Francis – but why is Chick getting involved in a big boys' fight?

Beating Martin Johnson and Ben Clarke . . . just.

Flying highest – what an outstanding number 8!

ollecting the Rugby
Players Association
Blyth Spirit Award.

With the
incredible
Russell Kelsey
(centre) after
his Twickenham
to Murrayfield
'sprint'.

© GETTY IMAGES / ANDREW REDINGTON

The European Tour professionals – and big Gav –
sporting my Doddie'5 tartan at the Scottish Open.

Scott Quinnell and I give broadcaster John Inverdale a good 'shoeing', as Jamie Roberts and Sam Warburton admire our footwork.

Yours truly with JK Rowling, a wonderfully supportive lady in the battle against MND.

Toon Army: the Falcons commemorative stri[p] for the Northampton game at St James' Park

When I came off second best to a coo.

Daft Vader.

The Weirs on Lions duty
in New Zealand.

TRY TIME! TRY!

The massed ranks of Scotland supporters aboard their flight to Italy
for the Doddie Gump March on Rome.

Being put on the spot by the lovely Gabby Logan.

Back at the Greenyards to launch the Trust and Foundation in 2017
(from left: Jill Douglas, Scott Hastings, me, Gary Armstrong, Kathy, Stewart Weir).

Tartan Giraffe Ball organisers Douglas Stephen, David Baird and Stewart Bennet
with hosts Jill Douglas and Dougie Vipond (far right).

Angus, Ben and Hamish accompany me onto the Murrayfield pitch ahead of the All Blacks game.

Kathy and I are honoured to meet Her Majesty with the Duke of Buccleuch.

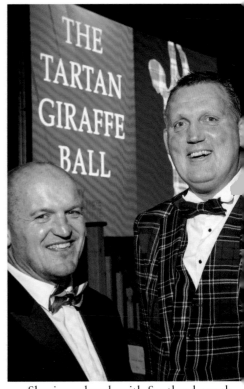

Testimonial dinner organiser Kenny Logan and comedian Kevin Bridges and me, backstage at Battersea.

Sharing a laugh with Scotland coach Gregor Townsend. We go back a long, long way . . .

Family affair: Dad Jock, me, Kathy, Ben, Mum Nanny, Hamish and Angus. We always dress like this on the farm.

So 'Too Tall' played and, just to land a real double-whammy on me, Scotland beat England on a sopping wet Sunday at Murrayfield and won the Calcutta Cup, something I'd never done during a decade of pulling on the dark blue jersey. I was chuffed.

Andy Nicol, with his bloodied chin (from an old shaving injury) lifted the famous old trophy, thus adding another element to this tale, as he only captained the team because my Falcons colleague, John Leslie, was crocked.

Scotland ended the season on a high and would pack their bags for the summer tour to New Zealand with a spring in their step. Or at least those who booked up for the tour would.

There were positives to be had by going to New Zealand. One being that it was always a privilege to play for your country; another would have been the chance to play the All Blacks again. While I think only Scott Hastings had more caps than me at that time, and though I never set out to break any kind of record, it would have been nice to have – especially as a USP if you were maybe planning a book. That was 2000. It hasn't taken me that long to get around to writing it.

However, I was giving serious consideration to missing that trip. I had sat out a tour to Argentina in 1994, simply because I wanted to rest up for what was going to be a big year ahead, and I did the same in 1998, to Fiji and Australia, entirely because of fatigue after the Lions, the knee injury and winning the title with the Falcons.

I'd mulled it over in my head for some time, and quietly mentioned it to one or two. They seemed to think my reasons were excusable. There wasn't any direct pressure being applied by Newcastle, none at all, but there had been a chat, which was not too far removed from my own thinking.

The other thing was that, ahead of the previous World Cup, I thought I'd suffered more knee damage in, of all places, Witbank, where I'd been kicked out of the Lions tour two years prior. It shook me up, mainly because it had been no more than a fitness exercise ahead of the World Cup, and I'd almost jeopardised all of that by being there.

Now, in the spring of 2000, I was left with a choice between another tour with Scotland or giving myself a rest to prolong my career. I think when you get to a certain point in time, the things that got you going – the excitement, and the energy that brings – are just not there to the same extent because you've seen it, done it.

When you are a younger player, as I was once upon a time, and Finlay made his comeback for the World Cup in 1991 having retired after the New Zealand tour in 1990, you ask yourself, why did he quit in the first place? Wasn't it great to play for your country, travel and go on trips and the likes? Of course it was.

When everything is new, and bright, and shiny, this international caper is simple and uncomplicated: play club rugby, get noticed, get selected, play for Scotland and enjoy. Then ten years into your own international career, you realise how Finlay must have felt in 1990, after several years with Scotland, then being captain of a successful Lions tour to Australia, with everything that would have entailed on and off the field, and then being an integral part of a

Grand Slam-winning side. That was why he said enough was enough.

Now the demands of the professional game, with domestic and European competitions, with summer tours of a sort almost every year, and the international Tests you would play in the spring and autumn, were really starting to take their toll.

That isn't even taking in to account staying fit, or, what is more challenging, getting back to health after you've been injured along the way a few times. The injury on the Lions tour is well documented. Recovery was tiring, both physically and mentally. I had then sat out the majority of the Five Nations in 1999 with a broken ankle. Once more, getting back to fitness, for a renowned hater of training, had been hard.

I therefore had a call to make, quite an important one, and I came down on the side of topping up the tank with a bit of R&R, and then I'd be flying again come the autumn or, better still, into 2001. But the Autumn Tests against USA, Australia and Samoa came and went. Nothing.

I was selected to play for Scotland against the Barbarians in 2001, but they didn't award any caps for the game. It doesn't, therefore, appear on my record, or in my thoughts.

What was interesting that day the Baa-Baas team was announced was that my brother Thomas was up on a disciplinary at Murrayfield, accused of stamping on Chris Capaldi's head during the Melrose–Boroughmuir Cup Final. Even the 'victim' said Tom didn't do it. I thought I'd throw my weight behind his appeal and act as a character reference. It worked. He got twenty-six weeks, reduced to twenty under appeal, which I was not part of.

But back to Scotland matters, and it was only early into the 2002/03 season, when I had already moved to the Border Reivers, that there was any hint that I had become a former international. Ian McGeechan had a cull ahead of setting up his training squad for the following year's World Cup. Some were told; others were left in the dark as to their fate. And some, me for one, had worked it out before Geech went public.

Like Kenny Logan, George Graham, Eric Peters, Andy Nicol, Gordon Simpson, Duncan Hodge and a few others, I'd be too old, as was the inference, for the next World Cup. Aged thirty-one? I was younger than Martin Johnson.

Like many things in my life, it wasn't the decision that was upsetting but the way it was arrived at and delivered.

All of which, of course, meant that the game against France back in 2000, when I trotted off to be replaced by my big Falcons pal Grimesy, was my last cap for Scotland, my last time on the pitch at Murrayfield as a player in a championship game. If I'd known, I would have made more of it, enjoying every moment, a bit like what I said previously about life itself.

And that's maybe why, in the most difficult of circumstances, I was able to savour and acknowledge the Murrayfield crowd in November 2017 ahead of the New Zealand game.

19

The Six Nations – the Toughest Test of All

FOR ME, INTERNATIONAL RUGBY was akin to going to war. You defended your territory, you looked after your colleagues and you did harm to the opposition. Not deliberately, of course, but in a full-contact sport, where you are intent on stopping opponents, or putting them on their back, it is inevitable that at some point in time you will hurt someone.

It would never make you feel good, but you ran the same risks yourself. Call it collateral damage if you like. That might sound hard, but rugby at the very highest level is brutally hard. It wasn't my thing, but I would never shy away if someone wanted to turn it into some kind of test of manhood or deliberately try and hurt me or a teammate.

That's why for the vast majority of the time, people play within the parameters, because of the respect you have for anyone who pulls on a jersey at the highest level of club or international rugby. You know what they've done to get there. For all those reasons, there is a bond and an understanding that I don't really think you get in many other sports.

That is particularly true within these islands, where most of us have clocked up the bulk of our international caps, in the Five Nations, and for me, the inaugural Six Nations season, against England, Ireland and Wales. Best of enemies and friends at the same time.

That said, I've been punched by Wade Dooley, who burst my eardrum and, in an instant, propelled me into the business class of international rugby, and by Martin Johnson, as well as umpteen Frenchmen. It's worth a mention, but different Scots, including international partners, also felt obliged to have a dig at me as well while in opposition. That was the game then. I always took it as a compliment, that I was doing such a good job and upsetting them so much that the only way they could get back at me was to lamp me.

However, it is safe to say that a great many players from the era when I broke through into the international set-up – in the early 1990s – may not have had a prolonged career at the highest level had today's directives and protocols been in existence. If they hadn't been sent off, they'd have been cited by one of the ninety cameras that cover a game today, then banned for goodness knows how long. Different rules then.

All of which added to the mix every spring, come the Five Nations. It is such a simple concept, but it works so fantastically well. Rugby just wouldn't be where it is today without this series. Never forget that. There was always an edge to these matches. No one ever wanted to lose a game, particularly against rivals just across a border or a stretch of water away.

If I'm asked who was the hardest player I played against while with Scotland, I think most people mean the one most likely to do you damage, physically. I'll be honest, no one scared me that much. If I was wary of anyone, it was more in terms of the level of performance I knew they were capable of, rather than their brute strength or physicality. Again, I could handle myself in that department, but the players who worried me most – and who I admired – were those who could run, jump and ruck all day, and had a bit of nous about them as well, those who thought about the game and could play it.

Let's start with the Auld Enemy. I touched on Dooley, or rather he touched on me, but his performance alongside Paul Ackford was like a light bulb going on in my head during that World Cup semi-final in 1991. Outplayed, and clueless how to combat it, I realised there was more to this international caper than met the eye.

You learn from your peers, and from those who have been around the block and come back for more. Martin Johnson and I are of a similar age, but I looked upon him as someone I could learn from. Simon Shaw and Garath Archer as well were bloody good players, teammates and opponents. Hard, demanding, and that went for so many English players at that time: Peter Winterbottom, Lawrence Dallaglio, Neil Back, Dean Ryan, Dean Richards, Richard Hill, Ben Clarke, Jason Leonard, Brian Moore. Add in there my old boss Rob Andrew, Will Greenwood and Jeremy Guscott, although the backs from any nation always spoke a different language to me and usually had a different perspective on the game and life in general too.

Some individuals, regardless of their nationality, had a higher profile than others, but my measure was always what I met on the pitch, and off it. The latter element is something I'll hark back to around today's players. Do they still enjoy that social element we did?

My track record against the English shows a one hundred per cent record – played eight and lost them all. Now that is consistency. Maybe it was because we knew the result before we ever started at Twickenham, even if we did go in with the best intentions, but it was a stadium that I never really took to.

I'd enjoyed a measure of success there with Newcastle, but even then, while it holds a lot of people, is a massive structure and I still go back there doing some of my corporate and media work, I just never warmed to the place.

Cardiff, whether as the Arms Park or the Millennium Stadium, or the old Lansdowne Road in Dublin, now they were different, possibly because you were within walking distance of the Angel and the Burlington hotels, respectively.

Lansdowne Road was the last of the old-fashioned stadiums, not touched by the legislation that had been introduced in the UK concerning sports grounds, and therefore still something different. You knew not much had changed since you watched Roy Laidlaw scoring down in his favourite corner a decade and a half previously.

I lost just once to the Irish, in my last game against them. Up until then, only a draw blemished my record. I don't want any of my Celtic colleagues to take this too badly, but the only nations I have a better record against in full internationals are Ivory Coast, Japan, Spain, Tonga, Samoa and Zimbabwe. So – thanks, lads.

The outstanding players of my generation would, naturally, include Nick Popplewell, Peter Clohessy, Keith Wood, Paul Wallace, Brendan Mullin, Brian O'Driscoll and Ronan O'Gara. But I played directly against a few legends as well, the first one being none other than Donal Lenihan. He was coming to the end of his career – it was time more than me who caught up with him – but as a young, impressionable pup, you couldn't help but be impressed by him as a stalwart of the Irish team, in much the same way as you viewed John Eales or Ian Jones.

Paddy Johns, Neil Francis and Malcolm O'Kelly, along with Mick Galwey, are probably the opponents I best remember. Like Scotland, the Irish had some superb operators, but it isn't always the big names that have caught my attention. For me, actions speak louder than words and even reputation sometimes.

I always thought Philip Matthews and Denis McBride, both flankers, were among the best players I'd ever come up against. When you look at someone and wonder how they seem to have been in two places at once, then you know there is something about them.

I only played against Philip twice, nearing the end of his career, but you could see he was special, and my Scotland teammates who had played against him a few more times than me rated him as well.

Denis McBride's inclusion has everything to do with him never being on the winning side against me in five attempts.

However, playing with that level of commitment, in a losing team, not once but every time, takes total commitment, which you can only admire.

Apparently, the stats say I only had a fifty per cent success rate against Wales. That could also compute as a fifty per cent failure rate. I'll settle for the former.

It goes without saying that Scott Quinnell was one of my favourite opponents, favourite people really. It cannot have been easy, growing up in the shadow of his father Derek, a Wales and Lions legend – look up his record to see how he qualifies for that status – but Scott tackled that with good grace and no lack of ability. Remember, what he did in a Welsh shirt earned him a contract in rugby league when that particular code only bought the best.

Second-row forward Gareth Llewellyn was someone I liked playing against. Uncomplicated, stood his ground, gave as good as he got. It doesn't sound a terribly sparkling recommendation, does it? However, for me, every time I played against him, he tested everything you had.

Remarkably, given everything I think about backs, I rated quite a few Welshmen very highly. Now, you may think one has been swayed by events around the 1997 Lions tour, but about six months prior to that I came up against arguably the best back division I'd ever seen in the Five Nations, and that is saying something: Neil 'Dead Eye' Jenkins at full-back, Ieuan Evans, Allan Bateman, Scott Gibbs and Gareth Thomas, with Arwel Thomas and Rob Howley at half-back. Just bucketloads of talent.

Scott, of course, took on the status of an honourable Scot in 1999, with his try against England at Wembley that won us the last Five Nations title. We forgave him for anything that had gone before because of that.

When reviewing the Five/Six Nations, we always seem to do it through a prism of comparison against the nations of the British Isles. Maybe it's because we have more in common with each other in terms of language, or where we play, or that every four years we all join up to create the Lions again.

By contrast, the French and Italians feel almost like add-ons. I won't dwell for too long on Italy. Played one, lost one was my championship record against them. France, though, were always the real deal.

Throughout my time playing Five Nations, and briefly Six Nations rugby, there was nothing the French could do that didn't surprise me. They could be the most ill-disciplined bunch who would collapse like a condemned house as soon as you applied any pressure to them, or they'd fight for every square inch, and have a back division that would attack and run from anywhere and with skills that would match any circus juggler or the Harlem Globetrotters.

Remember, there was a time when the French weren't household names. We didn't have satellite television channels showing dozens of French league games, and neither did we have European competition. We often only became familiar with French players during the period of a Five Nations Championship, or got to know them better if they hung around for a few seasons, which wasn't always guaranteed given how fickle the French team selection process could be.

They would happily pick three number 6s on the back

row, or play four locks. It was even more of a lottery among the back division.

Neither did we have the plethora of players shifting across the Channel to play, and therefore able to give us the lowdown on who to watch or what we were likely to see. It wasn't like when Toony, Tammy Trout, or wee Basil – who even has a French child (not as scandalous as it sounds) – were out there plying their trade.

The first one I can remember doing that was Damian Cronin, who always did a plausible impersonation of someone who might live in France. 'Del Boy' famously assisted Gavin Hastings with his captain's speech after our win in Paris in 1995. Big Gav had them crying with laughter, as he read out his prepared statement, penned by Damian, explaining how he had enjoyed some manly activities in the shower, before shaving his legs, and that he was indeed wearing his wife's underwear that night.

Perhaps just as well Del Boy wasn't asked to conduct too many spying operations.

That game was played at Parc des Princes, which was just a football stadium used for rugby. The atmosphere was pretty good, with an outstanding rendition of 'La Marseillaise' guaranteed. They cheated, of course, sticking microphones in among the military band to fill the stadium with noise, while our bagpipers just blew, unaided.

While the French possessed some of the best backs I ever played against, they still based their game plan and rugby model around their forwards. I can't recall ever coming up against a French team, in Edinburgh or Paris, and thinking that their pack looked on the smallish side.

They came in three fittings: massive, huge and ginormous.

They all had a similar look as well: unshaven, possibly unfed, freshly wounded around the eyes and the bridge of the nose from having spent the previous afternoon in a full-contact rucking session (hence why there was always a late call-up or call-off), looking as if they had only just completed fifteen years on Devil's Island with no chance of remission. Probably that's the reason they weren't the best socialisers after matches. What they were, more often than not, was brutally effective opposition.

In 1998, they rolled into Edinburgh and gave us an almighty beating, 51–16. In all my time playing for Scotland, it was as comprehensive a doing, to my mind, as we'd ever suffered, as they crossed for seven tries and completely dominated us up front.

To refresh my memory, I looked up that team we faced; the backs were Sadourny, Bernat-Salles, Lamaison – who nearly decapitated Craig Chalmers the previous year (when Chick joked he felt as if he'd been hit by a house) – Glas, Dominici, Castaignède and Carbonneau, while up front were Califano, Ibañez, Tournaire, Pelous, Brouzet, Marc Lièvremont, Magne and Thomas Lièvremont. What a team.

Of course, I mostly got to see who I was directly in opposition to. That day in 1998 it was Fabien Pelous and Olivier Brouzet (well named), having previously faced such players as Marc Cécillon, Olivier Roumat, Abdelatif Benazzi and Olivier Merle. Few who played against or saw them would forget them in a hurry.

As I may have said elsewhere, this book has been tremendous fun, particularly in seeing who I actually played against or, at least, who I was on the field with at the same time. If you just took a random position, say centre, I played against Philippe Sella and Franck Mesnel. How good was that? Tell me, please, I don't remember, other than we won.

I know the Lions have played the French in the past, albeit for a commemorative match. But I have wondered if there would be any merit in a short, three-match series against France at some time. Just an idea, but the way international rugby is progressing, anything is possible.

I think we've always taken the Six Nations for granted. It has grown in numbers over time, but it's when you see the Tri-Nations adding Argentina into the mix that you see just what a great championship – I think 'product' is the modern terminology – we have. The level of competition is fantastic, but so are all the peripherals, like the rivalries, the friendships and the camaraderie, among players and fans.

Things can always be improved. Talk of a secondary tier, and maybe promotion or relegation, or at least a play-off, to freshen up the competition has been around for a few years. But why change something that isn't really broken?

As it stands, we are privileged to have the Six Nations, and everything it brings to the game in the Northern Hemisphere. And to think there was a time when some would have put even that at risk.

Oh, I know people might point to some poor Italian performances and results, and question where they are headed. By the same token they could do the same for Scotland across a similar period, when we and the Italians contested the Wooden Spoon. They wanted it for their pasta, us to stir our mince. Would anyone want to lose the Scots? Don't answer that.

And, anyway, Rome of a spring evening I fancy might be slightly more romantic than Tbilisi at a similar time of year. Why not a Seven Nations? Maybe I'll register and trademark that.

20

Newcastle - Winners

THE LINK BETWEEN THE FOOTBALL and the rugby was pretty strong at the time in Newcastle, with Sir John Hall the conduit. It helped me, especially when I had my knee duffed up on the 1997 Lions tour. When I came back, I went to see a chap by the name of Rob Gregory, who was the surgeon who rebuilt Alan Shearer's ankle and looked after his knee at times as well. I was in very capable hands, and all down to the presence Newcastle United had in sport.

After a bit of consultation, Rob Gregory said that if you rest and leave it alone, it won't be any weaker than it was and we won't have to operate. That was the decision, and he was spot on. I rested up, then started building up the strength in my knee, and never looked back. I only have twenty-five per cent of my anterior cruciate ligament. The lateral and medial ligaments, they can heal, so it was explained to me that even if I had an operation to fix the AC ligament, it still wouldn't be any stronger than it was at that time.

I took two months out, and did some high intensity rehab, and was back playing for the start of the new season, which would begin with Bath, away, at the Rec. It was measure of the quality of what we would face during the 1997/98 term in the Allied Dunbar Premiership.

Like the Lions trip was the first of the professional era, so too, in my mind at least, could you consider the 1997/98 domestic season as the true starting point for the pro game. It is the norm today, but back then you could really feel that it was something special. Professionalism was by now fully embraced, and that meant every team had been busy recruiting and strengthening, either from within, offering their own players who had come through the ranks a deal, or through the emerging transfer market, or by raiding other teams for their leading lights.

There was no place for being moralistic, asking what this might do to rugby. Even without professionalism, players have always wanted to test and better themselves, playing at the highest level. Maybe the attraction of a pay cheque every month stretched loyalty, even commitment, and made it more important to some to play for the bank balance, not the jersey. It was where we were at.

But I never felt that's what was happening at Newcastle. Yes, we were handsomely recompensed for what we were doing (although it is small beer compared to today), but I always got the feeling that, to a man, we had all bought into the idea, plan and concept of turning the Falcons into the best team in England, even Europe. We did have some of the best players in the world at that time, but we also had a bunch of guys prepared to put their bodies on the line, week in, week out, just to achieve that goal.

Size mattered, whether that was in terms of the squad or

budget, and survival became a bare necessity. You were never going to grow if you couldn't stay among the big boys. That raised the stakes, which, like the investment, were massive. Every game would feel like a cup final. And, in late summer 1997, twenty-two cup finals beckoned.

Despite my injury in South Africa, I was fit for work come that August afternoon at Bath, with live TV, a full house, and Steve Lander, the man Popps had tried to assist the previous season at Bedford, refereeing. Thankfully, we kept a full complement on the field and won 20–13, although Deano did get involved in a bit of ill-mannered fisticuffs, as the late Bill McLaren might have described it. Always good to see your captain fighting your corner.

That day, the Bath team contained Perry, de Glanville, Catty, Ubogu, Nigel Redman – my Lions replacement – with Eric Peters lying in wait and Hilts lying on the bench. When we played them in the return game, in the May of that season, Bath had Callard, Ieuan Evans, Guscott, Adebayo, Nicol, Regan, Mallett and Balshaw in their team. Forget what I said about cup finals. Test matches would have been nearer the mark.

Still, it was the ideal start. Even Sir John weighed in with the celebrations. After Bath, we beat Northampton. Sir John disappeared off to Tesco and allowed us to buy a carry oot, which must have been the most high-brow carry oot of all time, paid on his gold card, or platinum card, or diamond-encrusted card. Very kind of him.

Popps was a cross between a school monitor, a prefect and a minder to us. As a wee pick-me-up to the lads – not that we needed too many of them – Sir John's son Douglas would slip Nicholas a few quid and say, 'Away and treat the lads.' But those gestures typified the family spirit within the club, and the genuine support from Sir John. Winners love winning, whether that is in business, life or sport. And it became a habit for us, although we had company for much of that season in the shape of Saracens.

We were neck and neck, but the race for the title took a turn over the festive period. On Boxing Day, Saracens lost at home to Leicester Tigers, while we clocked up fifty points against Bristol. Next up: Leicester, away. Looking back, if one game put a marker down that season, then that was it for us. Welford Road was a bit of a fortress. No one got it easy there. But we outscored them three tries to one, and kept the winning run going. That was another result that really registered with Sir John. Party on the bus? Don't mind if we do.

We went through all kinds of adversity, eventually getting to 12–0, before in match number 13, we faced Richmond. And it was unlucky for us. Still, it had taken until March for us to lose a match, hardly time for panic measures, and beating Saracens next time out meant we hadn't lost any ground.

But Sarries were a good team and got their revenge a few weeks later, only for us to lose again by a point that midweek, away to Wasps. The pressure was on, some of it of our own making. However, if it was hard going for us, no one else was getting it easy either. Saracens could only draw at Welford Road that Saturday and we went on a run of three successive victories – including two at Gateshead against Tigers and Wasps – leaving us one win away from the title, which we could claim in the last game of the season.

We had to beat Harlequins at the Stoop to become champions. I don't really recall being too nervous or apprehensive in the week leading up to the game, probably because we weren't the focus of attention in the toon that week.

Newcastle United had reached the FA Cup final and that was all that mattered for the vast majority in the North East. The city was decked out in black and white, top to bottom. I'd never seen anything like it, a measure of the football team being the real sporting heartbeat of the city. It meant that week we could just get on with our business and prepare for Harlequins, in the bottom half of the table, but unlikely to gift us two points.

That was on the Sunday. The previous day, United had lost in the final of the FA Cup, beaten 2–0 by Arsenal, and we'd gone along to see them. It wasn't the result anyone associated with the business wanted, particularly Sir John. It didn't put any more pressure on us to deliver, but neither did we want to let him or anyone else down. We need not have worried.

We scored six tries and, not for the first time, Rob Andrew had a great day with the boot. Indeed, he had a wonderful season, given everything he had to contend with off the field as well. Rob was a great guy, and still is. As a player, he was outstanding. His move into management, and the director of rugby role at the Falcons, was fast and fraught. Playing at that level was hard enough, but to also be team manager and team builder simultaneously was a feat and a half. And then he had to guarantee winning on top of that.

The stakes were always high, but his gambles paid off, especially with one in particular. Everyone at the club had become familiar with this kid who, a season or so before, had started showing up at training.

Jonny Wilkinson must have only been seventeen or thereabout when I first met him. He still looks seventeen. The only reason he has ever had a beard was to make him look older so they would pay him the adult rate on telly, instead of that of a child performer. Thinking-wise, and in terms of skill, he was way in advance of his years. He understood so much of the game, and the bits he didn't know, he learned, and as a number ten, had the ideal tutor in seen-it-all, done-it-all Andrew.

What was funny back then was the arrival of any youngster – the apprentices – in the team. In they'd come, into the dressing room for training, pick a peg, then be told to move, because such and such always sat there. So, the new wee laddies would eventually have to get changed on the floor, then after training, gather up all the towels and kit for the laundry. Some might see that as being a little bit cruel, though after a week we'd squeeze them in somewhere, so they got a peg. But what it did let them see was that just because you'd made it into the changing room didn't mean you'd made it. You had to earn your peg, which meant being there long term. Jonny embraced that apprenticeship period, didn't moan, got his head down and the rest is history. Imagine explaining to Sir John if he'd taken the huff and walked out.

Jonny's dedication and diligence put many – with me first in the queue – to shame. He was meticulous, just to get everything spot on, particularly his kicking, left foot, right foot. He was naturally a lefty, but how can you say he was when the most important kick of his career was delivered right-footed? That's how good Jonny was.

His routine, and concentration, was unbreakable. Clockwork. Tick-tock. Bang. Two or three points guaranteed. It is interesting seeing Cristiano Ronaldo taking a free kick, going through a similar drill. He doesn't do it, though, like Jonny did, thirty seconds after the French pack has tried to disembowel you.

If practice makes perfect then he was perfection. Afternoons, after-hours, would be spent practising. Place kicks, left side, right side, drop goals, touch kicks, left foot, right foot. If Jonny got a lot out of the game then it only mirrored what he'd put in.

Tackling and defensively, he put the hours in as well. He needed those attributes when at centre, but at number ten, he was often the first-up tackler.

The stand-off was, in many teams, the weak point of the defensive chain, the guy you targeted if you wanted to punch a hole in the back line or tie up loose forwards in midfield. But Jonny never shirked his duties – I can only think of Chick Chalmers in my time who was equally committed – in fronting up, even if you wanted to protect him and wrap him in cotton wool just because of what else he gave to the team, namely a cutting edge, or a barrow-load of points.

Jonny was my driver, as young players should be to their older, more experienced, better known, better looking, taller teammates, when the two of us lived out in Corbridge, until he moved to his palace, I mean place, out at Slaley.

An absolute dream to play with, and a wonderful person. He could have lived the Hollywood lifestyle, become the Beckham of rugby, lived off being the World Cup winner. But instead he just did more of the same that had got him to where he was. In today's sporting world, where people are promoted to superstar status because of the size of their contract, or for who they are dating, or what reality TV show they've appeared on, rather than how many medals they've won, I'm still full of admiration for what Jonny achieved and how he achieved it.

I've always thought in later years that Jonny was helped greatly by having Gary at scrum-half. Gazza would never just offload or throw him a hospital pass, one that would put Jonny under pressure or in any distress. Gary took a few hammerings because of that, but never took the easy play of tossing a hot ball to the man outside him. They were chalk and cheese, in terms of background, but identical when it came to the fight.

And Gary wasn't shy at standing his ground either. He has had many compliments along the way. *The Herald* reckoned he was Scotland's greatest ever player, which would tie in with Rob Andrew's considered opinion that Gary was the best scrum-half in the world when he signed for Newcastle. Jonny Wilkinson meantime likened Gaz to a junkyard dog, always snarling, yelping, wanting to pick a fight with his opposite number and, regularly, any number between one and eight as well. He had a switch. Others had it, where they are either off or on. Gary was never off, just on charge, getting ready for the next time. When he wasn't playing he was clowning around, then the laughing and joking stopped and he got stuck in.

Gary and I remain pals to this day, perhaps in some ways because we are similar, in as much as there may be a shyness to us. But where I can be quite an extrovert, Gary does his talking through his actions: leading by example, doing things his way and not taking any shit from anyone. Gary's career, in professional terms, was exactly the same as mine. We got something back out of the game, financially, as well as being part of a successful Newcastle squad.

The two of us sounded each other out on so many things. It is the same now. Nearly a decade and a half was spent playing with him. That's a lot of game time, training sessions, and car journeys together. And never a day went past without laughter and the ability to lead our lives the way we wanted – compared, say, to Jonny.

Most of us never had anything like the profile of Jonny. He was up there with the top footballers in the land, especially around Newcastle. But, as I've mentioned, having seen first hand what was expected of the latter, I wouldn't have wanted that either.

What was wanted in and around Newcastle, regardless of the setting or sport, was success. Sir John Hall didn't know the first thing about rugby, other than how much it cost. What he wanted was a winning team, and he wanted that across all the various sports he had a handle on, or a finger in.

He was delighted when we won promotion, and then celebrated like a good'un when we became champions of England. The only downside, which I imagine, being one of the owners, he would have been party to, was that the twelve Premier League clubs decided to boycott the European competitions the following season. They wouldn't compete in the 1998/99 season's European Cup and European Conference competitions in protest at the structure of the playing season, where a total shutdown of domestic rugby for four weeks in October and November, to play the European games, was something the English clubs wouldn't buy.

This was the second time I'd won a championship title – I did it in my last season with Melrose – and wouldn't get the chance to test myself against Europe's best because of decisions taken on high.

Some people might disagree, but I honestly think Newcastle would have had an unbelievable chance in Europe that season, had we been allowed to play. Unfortunately, we never got the chance to find out, and there was little point in getting all upset and emotional about it, because the task of defending the title, and of claiming more cups, was enough to keep you occupied.

While the league title was a terrific victory, I did always get the feeling that it was the cup competition that really appealed to Sir John. I think the drama and thrill of sudden-death, knockout rugby gave him a real buzz. Losing to Wasps at Twickenham in 1999 wasn't what any of us wanted, but we made amends two years later when defeating Harlequins 30–27.

That 2001 game against Harlequins was generally considered one of the best finals of all time. I was captain that year – they had finally realised my leadership qualities – but had been replaced during the match, so watched the closing minutes from the touchline, as we trailed 23–27 going into stoppage time.

Harlequins were not best pleased at the time when we were awarded a line-out with the clock deep into the red, especially when our prop Ian Peel appeared to be the one who took the ball into touch, but we got the throw-in. We then won the line-out and full-back Dave Walder managed to get into the corner for a score. And Jonny, unflappable as ever, banged over the extra points.

That win belonged to what I'd describe as the second generation Falcons. A lot of the big names had gone or were on the way out, and the local talent was in the throes of taking over. That was a facet unique to the professional game. Whereas in club rugby, if you were good, you could play until you retired, more or less, that option was now removed from us. Management, coaches, directors of rugby, owners: they dictated who stayed, who played, and who was nudged towards the exit.

Again, I didn't really have an issue with that. As a pro you had a limited shelf life, and no one was quite sure how long that window of opportunity would stay open. From my perspective, you couldn't just accept that someone had maybe made way for you, without being able to accept the same could – and most probably would – happen to you somewhere along the road.

The other thing to factor in was that the professional rugby clubs were now being run strictly on a business footing. Some of the big wealthy owners had moved on and weren't there to bankroll operations. Players who had signed lengthy and lucrative contracts were now a cost the clubs couldn't afford, or they knew they could get a better deal out there. By that I mean maybe two or three players for the price of one. The business side of sport had begun to bite. That meant tough decisions, and at Newcastle those would fall at the door of Rob Andrew.

Rob hired me, and steered me through the most fantastic time in my career, but ultimately he made the call of when my time was up. I wasn't upset; there was another opportunity that had become a realistic option back in Scotland, and I never had a cross word with Rob when the time came to split.

However, we might have, had things taken a different course a few years earlier.

After your first three years, you had to renegotiate the next three years. And I signed again for Newcastle Falcons. I was happy, settled and, as I've said elsewhere, pretty loyal. Newcastle had given me my chance, looked after me well, so why think about pastures new?

A good reason would have been money, and it wasn't because of a lack of interest or offers that I decided to stick, rather than twist. Somewhere, in one of the many boxes or files or kit bags I've squirrelled away, I have a contract offer from Saracens which at that time would have made me the highest paid domestic player in English rugby that season. Imagine.

Whenever we meet up, my agent at that time, Simon Cohen, now chief executive at Leicester Tigers, and I share a laugh together. Why didn't I sign it? What could have been? But I've never looked at things that way, and for the reasons given, I continued to love playing at Newcastle, despite being six figures down on what I could have earned. Ach, it was only money.

I am still in touch with Nigel Wray, the owner of Saracens, who was such a lovely guy when I went to see him; his magnificent memorabilia collection – and his television – were bigger than anything I'd ever seen at the time. His TV was like a wall. If only he had put the telly in the deal, that could have been a clincher. He and his family have been very supportive of me of late, and that for me is a real measure of the man. I was honest with him about where I was at, he accepted it, and me staying at Newcastle never came between us. And, to be fair, Saracens didn't do too badly without me.

But, having passed up on a chance to leave Newcastle by my own choosing, now, in May 2002, it was time to bid a fond farewell to the Falcons and English club rugby.

Inga, Pat Lam, George, Gary and me all said our good-byes at Gloucester. We'd taken a mauling, which didn't help the general mood, but I struggled to speak, Gary just coughed and spluttered, and as for George, I don't think he even showed face because he was so emotional. That's what Newcastle meant to us.

We were guys who had endured pain, put our bodies on the line, and given everything to the cause and now, to a man, we realised that our time was up. The brilliant teams, brilliant days, and the brilliant champagne and silverware were all over.

Thinking about it like that, I'm nearly shedding a tear now. But, remember, we had only ever gone to Newcastle for the money.

21

Back to the Borders

M Y RUGBY CAREER HAD BEEN a bit of a journey, but like every athlete in professional sport, you know at some point that this career will be no more – through age, injury, or just through having had enough of it all. None of those applied to me when my stay at Newcastle came to an end, so I'd play on, somewhere.

The opportunity with Borders came at just the right time for me. It was an interesting project, but one which probably didn't materialise the way I'd envisaged for a number of reasons. None of those details were, in isolation, that big. Collectively, however, it turned out to be the beginning of the end for my playing career. Maybe, in the circumstances, not what I would have wanted, or how I would have wanted it to finish, and certainly not how I saw things panning out when I came back up the road from Newcastle.

The Falcons adventure had run its course. Rob Andrew had some big calls to make in terms of how the Falcons were going to be run, and it became apparent that senior, big salaried players weren't going to be part of his plan. He had a business to maintain, and it was a business decision that meant Pat Lam and Inga Tuigamala left, and George Graham, Gary Armstrong and me headed home to sign contracts with Borders.

To be honest, Newcastle was great, but after six or seven years there, a change, or a new challenge, was needed, especially as my Scotland days were at an end. Hence why things played out quite nicely on all sides when Alastair Cranston, the chief executive with Borders, made his approach.

The notion of playing for Borders always excited me. First and foremost, coming from the area, and having spent all my formative rugby years playing there, I wasn't doing it for the sake of it, playing for any old team. It needed to have a meaning, some substance to it.

What better way to achieve that than playing for Borders. It was a terrific opening and an opportunity to keep my career going for another few years. It was a call that suited me, rather than others maybe dictating what I would do next.

Secondly, I'd always enjoyed playing for South District, and they had been a very significant force in representative games, in the old red and white hoops, although no doubt there will be someone out there, an anorak on Dulux paint charts, who will know the exact colour scheme: 'It's cherry and vanilla, Doddie!'

I was playing with some brilliant players from the seven Border clubs who all lent their colours to what has to be the most colourful tie in world rugby. Put it this way, it wasn't one you'd miss in a hurry.

But while the context was different, namely between a

select amateur team when I played in the 1980s and 1990s, against a pro outfit in the early 2000s, the quality of player was still going to be top end, with the guys who'd come up the road with me from the North East, and the likes of Gregor Townsend, who had spent the previous few years in France with Brive and Castres, waiting for us.

I'd known Gregor a very long time and, for me, his thinking was much the same as my own. If professional rugby came to the Borders – and we are talking about the area here – we'd want to be back there, playing.

The Borders team was new but, relatively speaking, so too were Edinburgh and Glasgow, nothing like the super teams they've become. It was a project, I felt, that was worth being part of and, I would say at the outset, Borders probably had a better base than the other two teams.

Arriving, it was all very exciting; the only downside for me being that we were going to be based and playing at Netherdale, in Gala. The rugby gods were getting me back. But, in fairness, they had spent a bit of money on the place, getting the pitch sorted out, and the facilities on the campus were excellent. It was also all part of a bigger, grand plan, involving Gala Fairydean and trying to get them into the Scottish football leagues. I think we are still waiting for that.

But a proper complex could also have given the Borders a venue for concerts and the likes as well. Again, sound calls and back then, all very exciting, and there was potential to grow, both as a team and into the wider community.

We didn't have to sell rugby to the locals. We needed them to buy into what we were trying: namely, setting up a super team to challenge in the Celtic League and Europe, not the

Border clubs which were, and still are, the bedrock of the game in that part of the country.

Tony Gilbert was installed as the head coach, a man with a significant CV, having played for Otago, and after his playing days were over, he'd moved up the coaching ladder to eventually coach the Highlanders and be assistant to Wayne Smith with the All Blacks. He appeared to know his stuff.

He would be assisted by Rob Moffat, who I knew well through his Melrose connection, and he and I went back to my time with Scottish Schools.

We were also quite a go-ahead club inasmuch as we were one of the first with a female fitness coach, Val Houston, who had played quite a lot of lacrosse for Scotland. Her brother also sells some rather nice cattle around Gretna. Maybe it was a combination of the two that kept me going. But she was very good, and very fit. When it comes to fitness and conditioning, you don't really want anyone who sent you out on runs then keeping up with you to make sure you did it.

We were trained hard. I've never minded that – I didn't always enjoy it, but it had to be done – but while there was so much onus placed on the physical side of the game, and preparation, I never got the feeling at any stage that Tony Gilbert was really on top of the game management side of things. Not what you would expect from someone with an All Black pedigree. However, I really didn't see the genius others talked about.

Every coach is different, but Tony was different to anyone I'd worked under. He put a lot of responsibility on to the players. Now, that is expected, especially around the senior players. But even then, there still has to be a bit of leadership given, determining the style you are going to adopt.

At Melrose, with Scotland, the Lions, Newcastle, the coach was always there to make fine adjustments, having first trusted each individual to do what was asked of them. That was never the relationship I felt I had with Tony. Perhaps I'd just been fortunate in the other places I'd played. Not that I think that, and I don't think one or two others would buy that argument either. There was just something missing, either in communication and how things were put across, or he was keeping his All Blacks playbook a secret.

For instance, when we'd practise line-outs, we'd end up calling our own drills. That doesn't work. Players end up arguing and squabbling over how many times you try something, and who you try it with. It's not the players who should be having those conversations with each other. In a match, fine. But not when you are trying to find the best, failsafe systems. And who tells you if it isn't working?

The hooker might have a different idea to the front jumper, or the guys at the tail, and the scrum-half might not agree with anyone, especially if you had a nine who was an argumentative sort. I bet you're already thinking 'Armstrong'. However, you can imagine some of the conversations that were being had, daily.

Yes, let someone make the line-out calls, let someone decide if we are going to kick or run, or take the ball forward through the forwards or the backs. But don't throw it open to everyone to have a say. Committees don't work in a match scenario, and neither does guesswork and, too often for me, that was exactly the state of affairs.

This was maybe when I started to look at professionalism a bit more cynically. We had coaches for everything. But the management and leadership, compared to how it had been done at Newcastle, particularly right at the top, wasn't there.

In the first season at Borders, 2002/03, we'd started out in the Celtic League with narrow home defeats to Connacht at Philiphaugh in Selkirk, and to Cardiff at Mansfield Park, home of Hawick. Back at what we had started to call home, at Netherdale, we beat Leinster and then thumped Glasgow. However, we lost all three away ties.

That Glasgow victory was a measure of what we were capable of but, in the grand scheme of things, it was they who made the knockout stages, and Borders finished with just two wins from seven. In Europe – in the European Challenge Cup – we ran in seventy-odd points twice against Madrid (you'll have noticed the difference between the rugby team from the city and the footballing giants of Real and Atletico), and then lost both away and home to Montauban.

It was disappointing, but remember it was just our first season. Unfortunately, the next campaign was even worse. A change of format to the Celtic League saw all twelve teams in one league (which would eventually become the PRO12), playing each other twice.

The intensity of such a demanding campaign, coupled with the fact that all three Scottish professional outfits were still finding their way as 'work in progress', meant it wasn't a great season for the Scots. Edinburgh finished tenth, Glasgow eleventh, and Borders, with just four wins in twenty-two games, were rooted to the bottom. We had beaten Edinburgh at Netherdale, but that was only minor revenge for them putting fifty points on us earlier in the season at Meadowbank. However, we'd taken some even bigger pastings along the way.

Some of that, to my mind, was because of the cutbacks and savings being plotted by the Scottish Rugby Union. Midway through that season, in December 2003, I began negotiating – as was pretty much the norm during my professional career – an extension to my deal. However, a stalling process began and, having been promised things would be sorted in February, February became March, which became April and then into May.

Tony Walker, now team manager with Exeter Chiefs, was someone I trained with. And 'The Beast', as he was known, helped me with something I'd never really been very good at doing, namely weights.

We used to train in the weights room, which was upstairs, but during those months of indecision, there were some days all he and I did was drink coffee and drop weights on the floor to make it sound as if we were training. I suppose you could say I was cheating. But, like so much of the way rugby was headed, I didn't see the point of having a card to mark up after every session as to how many kilos I'd shifted, or the number of curls, lifts and squats we had done, when you were guessing at line-out calls or didn't know what plays you might run.

There were a lot of good players around that time within the squad, like Ross Ford, Bruce Douglas, Scott MacLeod and Chris Cusiter. But the feeling of uncertainty within the group, about what may happen over the following year, led to a feeling of insecurity, and for me that manifested itself at game time.

Therefore, by the time the last Celtic League game against Munster came around at Netherdale, I was entirely resigned to soon being an ex-Borders player, although imminent retirement was still avoidable.

Japan offered a potential extension to my career, but having explored various paths and routes into the Japanese market, they eventually came to a dead-end. A good idea at the time, but no more than that. As a believer in things happening for a reason, just maybe, those rugby gods again were telling me something, probably that I was kidding myself on, and that the Man of the Match award against Munster – a bottle of whisky which I still have to this day – was no more than a farewell present.

Plainly, simply, during that second year, I just got bored and extremely disillusioned with the life being offered to me as a professional rugby player. Even big happy-go-lucky folk can be worn down.

It was not what I played rugby for, and I wasn't someone to just go through the motions. Training four times a day didn't excite me, didn't motivate me. I think that was over-looked, not just in relation to me, but some of the other experienced players who were at Borders. Was I suddenly going to become better, in my thirties, doing four sessions a day, compared to the player I'd been right at the outset, at Melrose, training two nights a week? No, that wasn't going to happen.

We knew what we were doing. What was really needed,

I believe, was to be kept as fresh as possible for game time, not having us fatigued, especially mentally. I don't want to sound as if I was looking for an easy time of it. Far from it. Find someone (other than Carl Hogg) who said I ever slacked and you'll have done well to find them. I was still giving it everything in games. But I was being worn down by the never-ending training, coupled to the politics, and a real fear of what the future would hold.

Having seen how things had gone at Newcastle, I was used to working within budget constraints. But the swingeing cuts, implemented at Borders, for me made it impossible for any high level of performance to be achieved among a squad that contained many young pros who were actually in the same boat as me, not knowing if their last paid day would come when the final whistle sounded against Munster. There was to be no second way either, an alternative offer or a Plan B. I would have been willing to stay on, to help develop the younger players. But that was not an option.

Japan, had it come off, might have been the jolt I was needing, but on reflection it would probably only have extended my malaise. I had bought into the idea of the Borders team, but by the second season, I really didn't want it. What it had said on the tin right at the outset in 2002 had become faded. You need to enjoy what you're doing, or why do it?

I'm not seeking sympathy now for something that happened well over a decade ago, and I didn't then either because there were things that would somewhat cushion that blow.

The boys, Hamish, Angus and Ben had all arrived while

Kathy and I had bought Bluecairn, a smallholding outside Galashiels. I was also about to take up a position with my father-in-law's firm, Hutchinson Environmental Solutions. I had something to fall back on – not that I had wanted to fall in the first place. Even so, suddenly having the 'former' and 'ex' prefixes, whether I wanted them or not, was going to mean a sizeable drop in income.

Despite the fact that I'd had an eye on the future, it still felt like a wee bit of an abrupt halt and a shock after what I'd been used to. What would I do now on a Saturday without rugby? Probably hide in case Mary Doll had plans for me.

And what began in 2004, with those funding cuts at Borders, was played out in full a few years later. The plug was pulled, and Borders were no more. Good while it lasted, but sad nevertheless.

However, by then, I was already off doing other things, one of the first being shooting a new series of *Superstars* for the BBC (who'd sent me to visit Santa in Lapland for *A Question of Sport* a few years earlier), out in La Manga, Spain. Amir Khan, Bradley Wiggins, Chris Hoy, James Toseland, John Barnes and Denise Lewis were all there, plus thirty other sportsmen and women. Skier Alain Baxter won for Scotland. I got a signed T-shirt.

22

Finding out There Is More to Life than Line-outs

B Y 2004 I HAD PRETTY MUCH settled on making the tran-
sition into the sewage and drainage industry, which
maybe tells you where I was at with rugby. Perhaps I'd
always been there. By that I mean that, despite it taking up
a huge part of my life and giving me a large chunk of it as
well, I wasn't totally dependent on the need to hang around
in the game.

Coaching would have been an option, but I'd seen perfectly
normal individuals lose their way just because of what the
pressure can do to you. Results as a coach are everything,
both in terms of your own pride and what longevity you
might have on the touchline. My heart was never really in
it, so therefore there was no disagreement between it and
my brain when it came to mapping out a new future. It
wouldn't directly be in the playing side of rugby.

There wasn't too much difference between farming and
drainage, other than my services were more valued in the
latter. I'm joking, Dad. Don't cut me out the will just yet. It

may appear that Kathy's dad, George, was being generous with his job offer. The reality, however, was blackmail on my part – if he didn't give me a job, I handed her back. I started on Monday the 17th of May, after the Munster match on the Friday.

The reality was that it was a way of expanding the business. George and Hutchinson didn't do much in Scotland, even though they were based close to the border. That meant there were targets to be achieved and there were things that had to be learned, much the same as if you're starting anything afresh – school, work, sport. As my full-time job, it needed to be learned rather sharp. However, to the outside world, namely those who didn't know me or weren't properly aware of my situation, I must have looked like an ex-rugger sort who had some spare time on his hands.

I had done a bit of media work, like newspaper columns, while I was playing, while I'd also had a season as captain of Newcastle, so I had to be on hand to say a few kind words here and there as part of the job. I'd also dabbled in the odd bit of broadcasting along the way.

But now I was being offered speaking engagements, either at corporate events or at rugby clubs. Me? Did they have the right person?

As I said, I had other things to fill my diary, but there was no use in letting these requests drift past, because they might never come around again. As I'm forever saying, try everything once. Richie Gray claims he suggested that I try the public speaking and after-dinner scene. Maybe I should credit him with something. But he said, get the suit on and give people your chat.

The first time I'd invested in a tartan suit was when I was in my late teens, along with Hoggy and Basil. Actually, I think I paid for Hoggy's. That's money I should be collecting for my old age. And some of us looked better than others.

I did have a couple of pairs of tartan trousers, but when I was asked to do some TV work up in Aberdeen, I got measured up for a full suit – in Aberdeen tartan no less – and that was the start of it.

After that came the Melrose tartan suit which I got for the Sevens. I think those appearances, more than anything, got people into the habit of seeing me sporting my tartan suit, and led to the many enquiries as to where I have them made.

The answer is I don't have them made – I have them built!

There followed the Irn Bru kit, the Lions suit – which is all four home nations, white, green, red and blue – and the now famous blue one, which I wore at Murrayfield last November (and may even have posed in for this book cover), and now the Doddie Weir Foundation tartan, which several of the Scottish European Tour golfers wore during the Scottish Open, a fantastic gesture from them and the Tour.

I'm very proud to wear the tartan. It identifies me, it identifies where I'm from. In other words, I am what it says on the tin.

I've now got about eight suits, which, contrary to popular belief, I don't wear morning, noon and night. It just feels that way. They are in as much demand as I am, so if I'm asked along to anything, there is always a request to wear a tartan suit as well. It's nice to be recognised as someone who has brought the tartan suit into the world of fashion, and it's amazing who has followed my lead. Prime Minister Theresa May was pictured in one, and then of course you have the guys who buy their own suits just to look the part at functions I attend, like Garath Archer and Stuart Grimes did for the Burns Night the Falcons had back in January 2018.

That's when you see the difference between one of mine, costing nearly a grand, and the examples they purchased online 'for just seventy quid', which looked as if they'd been sprayed on. They looked the part standing up – probably because they couldn't sit down in them.

That, then, is how we arrived at the instantly recognisable tartan suits. My problem currently is that, apart from my dinner suit, and my kilt and jacket, I don't have another suit to wear; well, at least not one that's fashionable.

I digress. Back to the public speaking and, despite the encouragement of Richie (and a few others), I wasn't so sure. But just so he'd stop pestering me, as he has no friends, I took his advice.

I should add that this would be around the same time as I was working with John Smith's, through one of my agents, on various public appearances around activities in Scottish horse racing, which was a great way of learning my new trade. I wasn't fronting the roadshows, so had a chance to see how they worked and get an understanding of why certain things had to happen in a specific way, because the sponsors were paying to get their message across. I even dressed like a jockey for a few of them, a very elongated jockey right enough. And this was where the tartan suits began to make more of an appearance, because I got fewer looks kitted out in tartan than I did dressed up as a jockey.

However, when I began speaking at dinners, I would have felt more comfortable in a suit of armour, to protect me from those staring daggers at me. What could be difficult about going to a rugby club and giving them chat? Quite a lot, if truth be told, as I found out on my very first engagement, at Consett Rugby Club. This had come a few years before, hence my reticence. I've never forgotten that night in Consett and, I dare say, the patrons may not have forgotten me either.

I was raking through a box recently and found my original speech, on how tall I was, how heavy, how much I trained, how many minutes I trained for, how much weight we lifted, what we ate, how much we slept. God, it read as badly as it must have sounded that night in Consett. Can I just say to their unfortunate – but supportive – members, that I am much better now and if you'd like to see me again, I'll come for just the beer tokens.

To begin with, it was quite nerve-racking, and something that wasn't easy for someone like myself who had struggled with shyness and a lack of self-confidence. The big, sticky-oot lugs, the above-average intelligence – sorry, I meant above-average height – and the fancy togs weren't going to be enough to survive. But rather than trying to match, copy or keep up with the comedians and professionals on the sportsman's dinner circuit, I soon realised that I had things they didn't have. Actually, they had things I didn't have, like timing, punchlines and a good memory. But that would come.

What I had was an insight in to the game they loved, the stories (or bits of them), the tales and the commentary and opinions they wanted to hear about the other players they admired or didn't, as was often the case. Once I started using my own material, it became so much easier, and because I maybe didn't worry as much, and was able to be myself and ad-lib from time to time, I became better and so it became more pleasurable. And I became busier.

I've spoken at lunches, dinners, suppers, working breakfasts, curry nights, coffee mornings and garden party teas. If it wasn't for people feeding their faces, I wouldn't have had a career.

You also get to meet the established guys on the after-dinner merry-go-round, and one of those is Scott Glynn, one of the funniest people you'll see or meet, who I've got to know quite well over the last few years.

Like me, Scotty has his own foundation, the Walk With Scott charity, which has raised some serious money – more than quarter of a million now – for good causes, not all of them the most obvious either. He identified that sometimes the simplest things – some respite for a carer, or just a night out for a family where one of the parents may be ill or incapacitated – can be priceless.

Big Scott has done so much of this work while seriously ill himself, which necessitated a liver transplant in October 2017. He wasn't going anywhere anytime soon, so I went and visited him in the high-dependency unit a few days after his op – in my overalls, of course. I was at work, wasn't I . . .

He was pleased to see me, so I planked myself down

on the bed to have a wee blether and eat his butterscotch crunch Border Biscuits. And very nice they were.

Not so nice, and not so pleased to see me, was the unit nurse, all of a foot shorter than me – about the same height as Kevin McKenzie (aye, that small) – who told me, 'Get off my bed and sit on that chair.' That was me telt – but it was worth it just to see my pal getting better.

Some of the places I've been asked to appear have been quite fantastic as well, sharing a microphone with house-hold names from TV and sport.

But three venues stick out as being particularly memorable.

Newcastle Falcons were good enough to invite me to host their hospitality at Kingston Park, and that was great being back among people who wanted to listen to me. We had some fun, particularly with the players and my spontan-eous three question quiz, always capable of embarrassing the most smart-arsed player.

Further afield, in 2014, I was entered into the Allianz Rugby Speaker of the Year competition, where I found myself in the final against fellow big boy Ben Kay – he who partnered Martin Johnson in the Leicester boiler room – and another Tiger, Austin Healey, the Leicester Lip (other nicknames are available but have been deemed unsuitable by the publishers). And I won!

I'd like to think it was my delivery and comedy genius that won it for me, although it could have been my Irn Bru tartan suit that dazzled the judges. Anyhow, that gave me a place in the final against Geoff Miller, the former England test cricketer and selector, and fellow Scot, from the world of football, Bob Wilson, who I have to say was an absolute gentleman. Scotland 2 England 1. The reality was, England won: Geoff was really witty and could spin a good yarn. Still, Rugby Speaker of the Year. That's been used on a few CVs and introductory letters ever since.

The other engagement that I always look forward to is closer to home. Having won sixty-one caps for Scotland, what an honour it was to become host on behalf of the Murrayfield Experience, entertaining up to seven hundred guests at all of Scotland's home Test matches.

That has been great fun, having many of my old colleagues and sparring partners up on the stage for a bit of banter. Occasionally, it has been fraught with danger. Handing John Bentley a microphone maybe wasn't the cleverest career choice I've made, I admit. I think we got away with it. There have also been a couple of, how can I describe them, near misses with some of the invited guests who I like to involve in proceedings.

Being six-foot umpteen, most people in my world are a bit on the short side. It means if I see someone short of stature, I do have a tendency to pick on them. However, that almost backfired spectacularly last season when I could only see a certain gentleman from behind and invited him on to the stage. I swear, I didn't know he was Chinese. But he took it in good spirit.

Similarly, how was I to know that the young girl who took part in the drinking game didn't drink? She could have said. Still, she made it back safely to her table and it only took a minute to replace the tablecloth, and the glasses, the puddings, the floral display, the chairs . . .

Those little moments, however, were not as difficult as

having to speak to the assembled gathering after the All Blacks match. It was an emotional day, emotion that, try as I might, I was unable to prevent spilling over into my closing remarks as I thanked everyone for a wonderful day. Thanks for putting up with my quivering lip and long pauses.

I've loved every minute of it, but like other things in and around the game, it's the meeting people that makes it worthwhile, especially when I can introduce a few of the locals into my routine. Thankfully, no one has been too upset at things I've said – well, not yet anyway.

The speaking circuit has given me an entirely new post-rugby career. It has also given me a bit of a soapbox, a platform, since my condition became apparent. Firstly to tell people what is happening and what is going on with me and, secondly, to prove I'm still here. People have suggested it also gets me out and about, and away from Kathy. But I couldn't comment on that, not when she's standing next to me, listening to what I'm muttering.

There are certain times of the year when you are in demand. For instance, at the end of the season, when rugby clubs generally have their awards presentation night, in January for the Burns Supper season (not a 'Haggis Night' as I've seen it advertised) and, of course, around the inter-national windows in autumn and spring.

I have to say, doing the dinner circuit has made me aware of just how many rugby clubs there are in the country, and how widely spread they are. Obviously you have your hotbeds of Wales, Scottish Borders, the Midlands and the likes. But I've been to some exotic places, from Cornwall to the very north of Scotland. And the good thing is, because they are all rugby clubs, I don't have to alter my routine too much. Actually, I don't alter it anyway, even if it's the Women's Institute or an army camp.

What is surprising is the amount of people who think that's all I do to make an honest crust. Far from it. That's just the showman, weekend dressy-up stuff.

Remember that sewage and drainage business, Hutchinson Environmental, that I mentioned a while back? That has been my job and my place of work on a daily basis since leaving the Reivers, in my role as co-owner, director, salesman, marketing and advertising guru, labourer, driver and any one of about thirty other posts I fill, to keep the business in business. Being a professional speaker would be great, but I've been happy with the work-fun split, even if it has changed in the last wee while.

If people are surprised that I have a normal job – or as normal as septic tanks can be – then many people I've bumped into up and down the land, in towns and more rural locations, have been shocked to see me. Assuming that is, they recognise me.

On one occasion, myself and my right-hand man, Lee Alexander, had been out on a job and turned up to help Stewart (Weir) get a big wooden playhouse into his garden. The only way to get it in was over a large hedge. I went on one side, lifted it up and over, with Lee and Stewart catching the panels on the other side.

Stewart's neighbour was quite in awe of my height.

'And what is it you do?' he enquired.

'I supply and install septic tanks,' I replied.

'What a waste. You could have been a basketball or rugby player . . .'

And, of course, my real job has seeped – keeping things fluid there – into my comedy routine, although some people do believe I'm making it up that I work in sewage for a living. Seriously.

But no. My one-liners – 'your business is my business', or 'your number twos are my number ones', and 'it might be your shite but it's my bread and butter' – are the reality of my life, daily.

The day I met Her Majesty during the summer of 2018, I had been inspecting a couple of tanks in the morning. Don't worry, I was all washed, steam cleaned and suited – well, kilted in reality – and booted for meeting the wonderful woman.

Kathy, however, was really nervous in case HRH asked, 'And what have you been up to?'

'Did you say twos?'

Thankfully I kept it in check. A few nights in the Tower didn't appeal.

23

Reality

NEW ZEALAND WAS A TRIP OF A LIFETIME. Any fit and healthy person would be hard pushed to better it. For someone like myself, with the old egg-timer running down (albeit with quite a bit of sand left in it), New Zealand, in so many ways the home of rugby, hosting the British & Irish Lions on tour, and playing host to the Weir tribe and associated hangers-on, was just sensational.

For me, even though I'd been to the land of the long white cloud before, this was still a once in a lifetime moment. Other times I'd been there was to play rugby, so while you did get to do a bit of the touristy things, playing the game came first. Being there without having to worry about matches and training getting in the way of personal enjoyment was just brilliant, particularly in the circumstances.

And then it was over. While out of the country we hadn't been entirely sheltered from reality but, for a large part of the time, it had been sweetened along the way. Boarding the plane and heading home, there was a feeling of trepidation; what would the welcome, if there was to be a welcome, be like? How would people treat us, and by us, I meant the entire family, because now that the news was in the public domain, Kathy, Hamish, Angus and Ben would be under scrutiny, and have as much to handle and cope with as I had.

All of those emotions were being traded off against a real longing to get home, to the farm, to the Borders, to business and normality, or whatever normality was to be from here on in.

The party was over.

To buy us a bit of time, a bit of privacy, just to gather our thoughts and plan what we might do next, we disappeared to our caravan for a week, down on the Solway coast, a place we'd been coming to since Hamish was a kid. There we would meet up with two old friends, Tory and Will Dodd. Kathy and Tory became friends when they were expecting, so they did the whole mothering thing together and since. Will and I were – and probably still are – bit-part players in the grand scheme of things and have become good friends through our love of farming. Actually, more our love of all things alcoholic, but we seldom mention it.

Our bolthole is pretty sacrosanct anyway. It has been a place where cares and worries have been forgotten about. In 2017, however, we really didn't want to be disturbed. Even though they were among the first people I had told, that homecoming couldn't have been easy for Will and Tory, seeing us for the first time since the word came out. It wasn't plain sailing for us either.

I knew things were different when Will started doing more of the chores around the place. He'd had a pretty bad accident a few years back when he came off second best to a coo – something I've had the 'pleasure' of a few times myself – and was pretty shaken up. But last summer, after watching me in action for the previous decade on how to be the man about the house – well, caravan really – and again even more so in the summer just gone, he really stepped up to the plate, barbecuing, washing dishes, going to the off-licence, all the important things on a holiday. So, well done to Will – I knew MND would be good for something and it appears to have embarrassed him into action. And, if you are wondering what the ladies do, nothing very much other than drink.

But we just love that location, and the times we've spent there. This summer was no different: lots of wine, Buck's Fizz, sun, late nights, later brunches. We enjoyed our summer break.

Twelve months prior, however, I wasn't even sure if I'd see it this year, so emotions were a tad more acute. Again, even while staying positive, you can catch yourself off guard, just by starting to look ever so slightly into the future.

The campsite gave us time to chill, relax, but at some point I was going to have to face day-to-day living again, as was everyone.

A lot of the time, I could be my old self, confident, bullish, taking ownership of situations where I could dominate the conversation, or steer it away from any potential 'chokers'. However, on occasions, you really were breaking up inside.

*

It was like that the first time we had a gathering of those who would, eventually, become the trustees of my

Trust, and later, the My Name'5 Doddie Foundation.

We gathered in Edinburgh, in the very plush surroundings belonging to the wonderful people who offered to look after the legal aspects of what we were planning. Sun streaming in the windows, a panoramic view out over the capital and beyond, making an ideal distraction for when the going went from good to heavy – distractions that in themselves could have you daydreaming the minutes away, until the reality of the situation and why we were there went off in your head like the one o'clock gun.

I'd hand picked my VII, all having unique qualities and an understanding of various skills and pieces of knowledge that would be needed to get my plans up and running. Scott Hastings, Finlay Calder, John 'JJ' Jeffrey, Gary Armstrong, Jill Douglas, Stewart Weir and Kathy were all there, along with a couple of the legal experts. It had to be done, but it was in many ways a surreal experience, because nice as these people were, friends for life for want of a better expression, they were discussing the probability of me not being there.

And while their intentions were good, and although their ideas were better, being asked, 'What would you want to happen?' threw me a couple of times. There was no chance of saying or asking to come back to something in a few weeks, not when time was of the essence, and so precious.

You can only stare out the window, or at the pencil in your hand, or at what you'd doodled, for so long. Then you would make eye contact with someone, and they wouldn't know where to look either. It was even harder when Kathy and I would catch a glimpse of one another.

I'd look at her, she'd look at me, and then the two of

us would be holding back the tears, or at least trying to. There was no point putting on a show or an act for these guys. They, themselves, had been at the emotional end of things from nearly day one. Privately, one or two admitted afterwards that was the moment when, to paraphrase one, 'The shit got real.' No more sugar coating, sprinkles, chocolate sauce. This was the harsh reality of planning for a future that would involve me, for how long we didn't know, but would eventually continue without me. It was an impossibility for them to discuss things fully, almost as if I wasn't there. That, though, was the reality of the situation.

I will say this honestly, but just like it had been with my family, I don't think we would have been able to even get moving had it not been for the support, emotionally, from those guys. They gave of their time, skills, patience, contacts, love.

It was touching and I couldn't help but think, *Why couldn't they have been this nice before?* Seriously, they were just incredible in those early days, and have been ever since. They say that you get to see the real person in times of crisis and adversity. And they are fantastic individuals, as are a few others.

What was also incredible – in fact, it was utterly staggering – was the level of support coming in from the wider community, either in offering time, expertise, or most unbelievable of all, financial help.

This was something the big dumpling from Blainslie just didn't foresee, or understand. I might refer to this many times within the next ten thousand words but the generosity of people has been staggering, and all of it based on folk being touched by either having seen me play (and there were times when people would have happily paid for me not to have been playing), or having seen me on TV or in the flesh at a function, or because of my plight. I say I get it, but I really don't.

It is truly humbling; there is no other way to describe it. If there was a way to raise funds, then people thought of it: a tractor rally with more than one hundred tractors at Thirlestane Castle, sponsored walks, sponsored runs, sponsored swims, sponsored clay pigeon shoots, sponsored cake making, cake eating, beer drinking, auctions, dinners, lunches, teas, curry nights, raffles, guess the name of the teddy, the bear, the lion, guess how many peas, Smarties, pennies were in a jar. Guess the name of the Smarties in the jar.

The ingenuity of people, to procure pounds, capture cash, or collect cheques, was absolutely astonishing. As was the age range of those involved, from school kids who would never have seen me play, to the golden oldies who had and still forgave me for never beating England. Actually, many of my English neighbours, friends and brothers were equally generous, probably in thanks for me playing my part in Scotland teams that never defeated the English.

I was never going to hide having been diagnosed with MND. I was going to fight it, and would be entirely public in doing so. But even I underestimated how busy I'd be, supporting the people, the rugby-playing, rugby-supporting fraternity, and the wider public across the country, as they supported me.

What brought it home was at the first meeting of the

trustees group in Edinburgh. There was a list of people asking permission to stage events and fundraisers, and Scott, Jill and Stewart had countless requests for public appearances, speaking engagements and interviews. And then when we got around to 'any other business', JJ produced cheques and cash, asking, 'And what will I do with this?'

This was quite staggering. We hadn't formally set anything up, as we'd been away, but already we were being supported from afar. That was very moving; there isn't any other word for it.

That was just the start of it. It has been pretty non-stop, difficult at times, and some days are harder than others just because of tiredness – although that isn't down to my condition, as some of my relatively fit and healthy cohorts have also found the schedule demanding. But I'm not complaining. It is all for a great cause, and not just my cause.

As I said, I was never going to shy away or be secretive about MND. But, suddenly, there was much more to contend with. There were still things that Kathy and I hadn't really discussed in full, but now we also had this huge outpouring of generosity and public spirit that had to be dealt with.

I'll be honest, some of it was a bit of a blur in those early days. That has become apparent when putting these words down on paper: being reminded, constantly, of various things, being asked to be in different places at the same time, if we'd be interested in doing this or that. I'd forgotten some of it, simply because there was so much going on.

Thankfully, the team we'd surrounded ourselves with

dealt expertly with the requests for appearances or interviews. I couldn't do everything. I thought I could, but it would have been impossible to visit or attend all the places and people that wanted to see me. I'm sorry to those who have been disappointed, but I think most have recognised that my popularity has risen of late, and my services have been in demand.

Back in the summer of 2017, we had started to tie up all the threads and leads, and had a game plan as to what we wanted to do, regarding the charity work, and how my diary and media requests would be handled. There were quite literally hundreds of those.

But a date was put in the diary to announce the setting up of the Trust and the Foundation: the 28th of August. The announcement would be made at the Greenyards, Melrose, which later that day would be hosting a pre-season match between Edinburgh and Newcastle Falcons.

We needed to get the word out about what we were doing, and I needed to tell people what I was about. I'd not spoken to anyone or any media outlet since we came back from New Zealand, apart from an impromptu interview in Edinburgh with Rob Robertson of the *Daily Mail*, who spotted me opening the Scotland Shop in Queensferry Street and popped over for a chat, which, Rob might not thank me for saying, went largely unnoticed and, therefore, didn't take anything away from the big announcement we had planned.

However, I wasn't entirely comfortable with facing what might have been the massed ranks of the media, newspapers, TV and radio. It had been fine as a rugby player;

win, lose or draw, and you were expected to fulfil your media duties while with club or country. But this had the potential – maybe make that the guarantee – to be beyond anything I'd ever faced as a player or pundit.

Our story needed publicity, yes, but while a couple of months had passed since the big announcement, there was still a rawness to the situation. Keeping your emotions in check, or hidden, wasn't the easiest of things to do.

Having talked things over with Stewart and Jill, who would be there on the day, the solution would be a pretty easy one and they took me through it. We would only invite a couple of photographic agencies, who cover sport and rugby in Scotland, and the three main TV outlets, Scottish Television, BBC Scotland and Sky News. They would send cameras and then share footage from the various and different angles. All very civilised and, I must say, they made it all as simple as possible in the circumstances.

The newspapers would get a transcript of the interview the following Monday when the broadcasters would release their footage and online interviews.

I was pretty confident that I could cope with just speaking to three people, who would be Rona Dougall from STV, who I knew from having appeared on *Scotland Tonight* a few times; former Scotland and Lions number 8 John Beattie, who, again, I knew through our TV and radio appearances together; and James Matthews, who I really only had seen on Sky. We were all set.

However, as we travelled to the venue, James sent an urgent message to Stewart saying he'd be unavailable. He was the only man on in Scotland that day, and his chiefs in London had dispatched him to a major, breaking news story. A political scandal at Holyrood? An incident in Edinburgh? A Hollywood superstar filming in Glasgow? Or was the President of the United States, Donald Trump, playing golf again at one of his Scottish courses?

No, James was forgoing interviewing me to set up camp at Edinburgh Zoo where Tian Tian the panda was believed to be pregnant and could give birth at any time. I had been second best on the rugby field a few times, but only to some of the greatest players of all time. I had never, ever, come second to a panda.

However, while there was a no-show from any baby pandas in the capital, our show had to go on.

I was glad it was Rona and John who did the interviews, people I knew and liked. Had it been complete strangers, or the massed media corps, in hindsight it would have been very, very tough. Not that it was easy for John and Rona. Voices broke, tears ran, I choked up, was consoled by Rona and John, then they'd well up, and I'd console them. There was a take two or three in among them.

It was raw, extremely painful, but they got to ask the questions they wanted, and I got to get my message across. Job done, there was even a kiss and a cuddle from Rona and a hug from the big yin. Who says this MND doesn't have its perks?

The newspapers also had a fresh angle on events come the Monday, but what happened when the TV footage went live was breathtaking, especially with the BBC's output, as you might expect from the biggest broadcaster in the world.

I had an alert set on my mobile phone, back working

again after its little holiday, which sent out a ping every time something was tweeted. By mid afternoon, the sound had been turned off. That ping had become non-stop, as messages, replies and retweets just kept dropping all day, all night, and into the next day.

John began texting me, giving me a running total on how many views the video had received on the Beeb's website. It was going up by a hundred thousand at a time. Was I that popular or famous – or infamous? It appeared so.

STV broadcast their interview in full later that night. Again, the feedback was astounding, especially when Rona gave me a hug at the end. I think her actions made the interview a very real thing, with people saying how nice it was to see someone conducting an interview reacting with such warmth and emotion and, in effect, giving me a much-needed cuddle on behalf of all those watching at home.

The next day, the newspapers added to the impetus. The ball had well and truly started rolling.

24

Fun and Funds

EVEN BEFORE WE HAD FORMALLY discussed the setting up of the Trust (which was to assist me and my family directly), and the Foundation (whereby I could put money into research and helping other MND sufferers), and what they might be used for, people were formulating plans to stage some major events to help me, so that I might help others. The first to donate was John Jones of Hitachi Construction Machinery, while one of the first to pledge his assistance was Kenny Logan, who had plans and ideas, already at an advanced stage of readiness, to hold a gala event in London. That was where Kenny's business was based, so he knew the market and, equally, knew the support out there that could be harnessed to help us.

Kenny, being Kenny, was full of enthusiasm and I'm sure, through his connections, especially with Wasps, that eagerness rubbed off on others. From giving him a green light to stage it on our behalf, Kenny put together, in the space of just three months, a star-studded celebration of my career.

Having started with a target of around 500 guests, that

figure rose progressively – 750, 800, 1,000 and then 1,200 before, with the Battersea Evolution bursting, the limit was set at 1,300 guests for the Doddie Weir The Good, The Bad & The Extremely Ugly Testimonial Dinner.

While I had played in many teams, three were selected to be the focal point of the night: the 1997 Lions, the 1998 Falcons championship-winning team, and Scotland's 1999 Five Nations Championship side, the one I had played such an important and starring role in (as you will recall from previous chapters).

We had enjoyed a long weekend away, starting with being flown by helicopter, thanks to my neighbour Danny Sawrij of the Leo Group, down to Jill and Hoggy's abode, and then on to see Worcester Warriors take on Sale Sharks in the Anglo-Welsh Cup. Not a good night for Hoggy, then head coach of the Warriors, as his team was beaten. Worse still, I found some great gear in the boot of his car – hats, big anoraks, body warmers, fleeces – and helped myself. Really good gear. I still have most of it. And from there it was on to London.

I turned up on the Sunday as they were building the room and the set. The building was huge. 'And we are going to fill this?' was my first question. Kenny had been confident from the off, but it did look awfully big. But what did I know. Next time I saw it, on the Monday evening, the venue had been dressed up and looked utterly amazing. Now, I wouldn't say that I became nervous, maybe slightly appre-hensive, and while not emotional, it was difficult to put all of this together: that this venue was a sell-out because of me, because of where I was, because of what I was trying to achieve. I didn't think too much about that, or dwell on it for too long. It was just difficult to put all of that into some kind of context.

This was a major event in what eventually became a year of big occasions, so by the Monday afternoon, the entire Weir tribe and the trustees had descended on the Big Smoke. However, there was business to be done.

On the afternoon of the dinner we were all at a meeting of the trustees, all except Jill, who was away covering snooker somewhere exotic like Hull or Rochdale. There had been a tremendous amount of work carried out on our behalf, especially by our solicitors Addleshaw Goddard, who, I have to admit, have made the legal, tax and charitable aspects of everything we are doing understandable and comprehensible to even the eejits among us, like Stewart and Gary.

JJ, who, as I was to find out, had obviously commissioned someone to write a rather nice welcome in the testimonial programme, then stuck his name on it, turned up with all sorts of paperwork that the trustees had to sign and have witnessed, which they duly did. But we needed to have an independent witness. Who to ask?

And at that point who should walk into the Tower Hotel but Brian Moore, ex-England and Lions hooker, along with his producer Abi, who had come along to record a piece with me for his *Telegraph* podcast. Handshakes exchanged, JJ thrust a pen into his hand and explained exactly why he would need it.

Brian sat down, spread the papers out in front of him, and was about to start signing when he looked up and around the table, at each of the Scotland legends in front of him.

'If I had ever thought I'd be acting as a witness for you bunch of bastards when you were kicking the shit out of me . . .'

'Oh, just f***ing sign them and stop your moaning,' Finlay intercepted, as a former Lions captain would.

Then it was on to the big night itself, seeing plenty of old pals, colleagues, teammates and best of enemies: Keith Wood, Mike Tindall, Rob Andrew, John Jeffrey, Finlay Calder, Scott Hastings, Gary Armstrong, Matt Dawson, Kyran Bracken, Gregor Townsend, Nick Popplewell, Paul Wallace, Martin Johnson, Stuart Grimes, Garath Archer, Alastair Kellock and Kenny Logan.

And Jonny Wilkinson, Will Greenwood, Peter Scrivener, Damian Cronin, Nigel Redman, Jim Hamilton, Phil Vickery, Jason Leonard, Brian Moore, Max Evans, Eric Peters, Bryan Redpath, Rob Wainwright, Jonathan Webb, Anton Oliver, Justin Marshall, Scott Quinnell, Craig Chalmers, Dean Ryan, Ieuan Evans, Jeremy Davidson, Kevin McKenzie, Gordon Bulloch and Richard Hill.

Then there was Michael Dods, Carl Hogg, Peter Walton, Adam Jones, Graham Rowntree, Robert Jones, Derek White, Chris Paterson, Budge Pountney, Jamie Noon, Lawrence Dallaglio, Sean Fitzpatrick, Rory Lawson, Simon Shaw, Derek Stark, Andy Nicol, Neil Back, Greig Laidlaw, Damian Hopley, Sir Ian McGeechan and Jim Telfer, of course.

Forget Test Match rugby. You'd take on an army with those guys. What a collection of talent. Sorry if I missed anyone.

Oh, but I have forgotten Gavin Hastings. Probably because

he wasn't there, but Rory Bremner did such a wonderful impersonation – and an equally great job as co-host – you would have thought the big man was in the room.

Then it was my turn. Take a deep breath, all your friends and family – Mum, Dad, Kathy, sons, brothers, brother-in-law, nephew – are here, and you'll be fine. Except, as I climbed up on the stage to be welcomed by the lovely Gabby Logan (she obviously sees things in Kenny that none of the rest of us see in him), there was a real feeling that holding it together might be a tad difficult.

Gabby couldn't have been nicer. However, and this wasn't her fault, I was struggling to answer the questions. Not because they were difficult, but they were just hitting the emotional buttons that I've tried so desperately to keep hidden. She wouldn't have known, but I did, especially when my boys came up on the stage.

I could have done one of two things. Welled up and got all upset, or take the conversation in other directions. Armed with my own microphone, I decided to get a handle on the situation.

I invited my brothers, Thomas and Christopher, on to the stage. Once I'd finished with them, it was time to get some of the big boys up: Jonno, Buzz, Grimesy, big Al. Then an unwilling, I mean unsuspecting, victim. 'Where is Kevin McKenzie?'

And with that, I had a full complement, bouncing jokes and one-liners off each of them, many aimed at Kevin. He'd been the brunt of my tomfoolery before. Don't tell him. He will be again. But the wee man took it brilliantly and helped make what could have been a real toughie moment into the beginning of a night of tales and laughter.

There were a lot of nice things said about me that night. I almost didn't recognise myself. The real laughter, though, came when Kevin Bridges came on. He had the place in tears, especially when a wag in the audience decided to join in.

Firstly, you never take on someone with a microphone. Secondly, you don't take on one of the country's best comedians, especially one from Glasgow. And thirdly, you don't do it when you have a public school accent. Poor chap, he won't do that again. He got absolutely, and unprintably, slaughtered!

The array of auction prizes was quite spectacular. One, in the silent auction, caught my eye: a 1946, 26HP, narrow front John Deere tractor. Now, you might not get terribly excited by that, but for me, this was the ultimate prize.

Myself, Gary and Hoggy put a bid together, three grand each. (Unfortunately, someone bid a whole lot more.)

'I didn't know you were into your tractors, Gary?' he was asked.

'I'm not.'

'Why did you get involved in this consortium then?'

'As an investment.'

'An investment?'

Gary elaborated. 'Well, if our bid had won, I'd have had a third of a tractor. But in the future, I could own half of it.'

Remember that black humour I mentioned. It can be ruthless, but I wouldn't have it any other way, even now. Some people might be shocked, or get offended on my behalf, when they hear some of the things said. But I'd have been open to it if I didn't have MND, so why should MND give me any kind of immunity to some of the banter that goes on, often at my expense?

The night will go down as one of my best ever. Just seeing so many people I knew and had played with, and to now see what they – in particular, Kenny and the testimonial committee – were doing for me, was an extremely humbling and emotional experience.

But I had better get used to it, because there was more to come. I was in demand, and the demands I placed on myself maybe didn't help. Anyone who was having a fundraising event, I felt like I needed to be there. The impracticalities of that soon became evident. Fine if there was a cheque or a donation being presented in Lauder at lunchtime, and maybe an event in Peebles or Dumfries later, or even Glasgow or Edinburgh at night.

However, when there was something in Cardiff, Oban and Yorkshire all happening at the same time, on the same day, not even I have the power of time travel or access to a helicopter 24/7.

I really wanted to make the effort. To prove that I could do it, and so as not to let people down, because I appreciated just how much they had gone out of their way to help me and others.

It wasn't easy to say no, far from it. I felt the disappointment that others would feel. But in terms of the sheer practicalities behind my workload – day job, speaker, ambassador, the face of the Foundation – it was impossible. And that didn't even include quality time with the family.

And yet I still tried to juggle all of those things. It only became workable when someone took the balls away, so to speak, and even then I'd still take on things at short notice – for instance, being asked to make the Scottish Cup draw. Having done it, can I tell all paranoid football fans who might be reading this that all the balls are the same – no hot or cold balls.

Then, last minute, we were going to the BBC's Sports Personality of the Year awards in Liverpool, which was such a wonderful experience for all of us, because we went as a family. Gary came along as well, and we met up with Kenny Logan, freeloading as Gabby's driver.

We got to meet legends and superstars. I had a chat with Kenny Dalglish, Michael Johnson came and said hello and the boys had their photographs taken with him and Anthony Joshua. It was great for them to take time to approach us and talk. Even Kathy got to pose with Carl Fogarty.

'I didn't know you were into your superbikes, Mary Doll?'

'I'm not. He won *I'm A Celebrity . . .*'

Every day is a school day.

★

Two dates that were set in stone came at the end of January and, as if to typify the demands made on me and everyone involved in the Trust and Foundation, they came just a day apart.

The first one was the Haggis Hike, the brainchild of Stuart Grimes, who thought it would be a good idea to have a Burns Supper at Kingston Park, and that for authenticity we needed a freshly caught haggis – 'a genuine Scotch haggis' as Micky Ward described it, although I was unaware of them breeding anywhere else.

But if you are going to all that trouble to capture a haggis, and then stitch it into a rugby ball for safe keeping, then why not add to the fundraising potential by marching it back to England. And that is exactly what they did.

Stuart, Micky and Gary were joined by Dave Walder, Garath Archer, Simon Best, James Cartmell, Pete Massey, Jim Naylor, Ian Peel and Michael Stephenson to make up the raiding party. Even Marius Hurter – who at the supper would sport the loudest tartan jacket I'd ever seen – flew over from South Africa to join in as the team tackled over fifty arduous miles of rugged terrain and winter weather, marching from Jedburgh to Kingston Park in just two days.

Me, I was flying back from America or I'd have been there for the lads – well, for the last four miles from Ponteland at least – if I hadn't been to the USA with former Sale Sharks owner Brian Kennedy in his private jet, an uneventful trip apart from having to land in Canada to purchase more whisky. Brian is another who I am deeply indebted to for everything he has done to help me and my condition.

A mighty effort and a fantastic night when many of the Newcastle players, fans and supporters were treated to some Scottish culinary delicacies and a bit of culture. Meanwhile, those who took part on the hike were treated in hospital for blistered feet. And some of them needed it.

The following evening, we were back over the border, if

only just, in Kelso for the Tartan Giraffe Ball, being held at Springwood Park.

I'm not sure who could lay claim to stitching my favoured cloth and Bill McLaren's famous description of me together to come up with Tartan Giraffe, but it was clever. The ball itself was the brainchild of Douglas Stephen, Stewart Bennet and David Baird (assisted by David Ferguson on comms), although there was some scepticism about their offer and their ability to stage something quite this big. I mean, they were, after all, from Kelso, and getting fifteen folk in the same place is considered something of an achievement in those parts.

Joking aside, what greeted the guests on the night was a spectacular transformation of the Border Union Agricultural Society venue. As Gary observed, tongue in cheek, 'Whaever did this cannae be local.'

Not that he could talk about style. The wee man had taken such a battering that he'd turned up in his dress jacket, bow tie and tartan trews wearing a pair of Crocs and virtually unable to walk, let alone dance.

And when the formalities and auctions, wonderfully managed by Jill and Dougie Vipond, were over, dance we did, the music provided by no less than former Scotland and Lions number 8 John Beattie and his band, and then for one night only, on stage, in Kelso, the fantastic Deacon Blue. The wow factor just went up a notch, as did the fundraising.

A few months later, Stewart, David and Douglas turned up to present two cheques: one to the Trust, the other to the Foundation. The Trust benefitted to the tune of £100,000, but the Foundation was rewarded with a staggering £210,177.

Utterly amazing amounts and I am eternally grateful.

However, this is where everyone needs to see a much bigger picture. Those big-ticket events have and will continue to raise sizeable amounts. But all the rest of the fundraising that has been going on is no less important, gratifying or emotional.

I went to Cloverfords Primary School – my sister's kids are there – and they were going to make a presentation to the Foundation, having raised £800. The school my brother Tom's kids attend, Stow Primary, raised £500. The kids were all smiles, all cheering, and all proud as punch that they were doing something to help me, the Foundation and MND sufferers.

It is brilliant, but trying to keep your emotions in check when you see the kindness of wee kids like that is difficult. That applies across the board, on a daily basis.

However, what the kids were doing was playing just as big a role in the fundraising, to try and assist MND sufferers, or to find a solution or cure to the condition, as anyone else.

Who is to say that the breakthrough might not be found because we have managed to fund an additional week, or a day, or even an hour of research?

Thus far, we have raised well over £1 million. One million quid. I don't know what our target was when we started out, but that is a tremendous effort from all concerned.

I'm not sure what that equates to in terms of raffle tickets sold, cups of tea, cars washed, cakes baked or auction prizes donated. What I do know is that I can never thank everyone enough for everything they have done and will continue to do in fighting MND.

25

Money Out, Me Out
and Still About

UNDER NORMAL CIRCUMSTANCES, I'd imagine that if I had a seven-figure sum in the bank, I'd spend most days looking at it. However, that is not what the money raised for the My Name'5 Doddie Foundation is for. It is there to help finance MND research and assist fellow sufferers.

None of the trustees ever considered or claimed to be experts on where the money would be best invested. It was important then that we sought counsel from a number of experts as to what course of action we should take. Having held our first advisory panel in April 2018 to learn as much as possible about current thinking and research into MND, we subsequently decided to contribute £400,000 to support the work of Chris Shaw, professor of neurology and neuro-genetics, and his team at King's College London who are investigating gene therapy for sporadic MND.

In addition, the Foundation gave MND Scotland £100,000 and a similar figure was committed to the MND

Association for England, Wales and Northern Ireland. Another £300,000 is earmarked for other projects.

As a body, the Foundation's trustees had made a number of donations to various individuals and families who had contacted us for assistance. I think, speaking for everyone involved, that our expertise wasn't in assessing or justifying who was most in need of some help and assistance. How can you compare someone in need of a wheelchair, against a carer desperate for respite, or a family requiring modifications to their home?

Collectively, we felt it better to allow those working with MND on a daily basis to make those calls, hence why we were happy to support MND Scotland and the MND Association.

All of which allows us to get back to fundraising, supporting events and for me to have an ambassadorial presence on the various activities and events.

Remember, everything I had been told suggested that by now, in the late summer of 2018, I would be finding day-to-day living virtually impossible, and certainly would not be an active participant in as many things. Time then to prove a point or two.

At the end of July 2018 I went on a Land's End to John o'Groats car run. Me, Richie Gray – that's the Gala one, not the good rugby player one – along with Alister Scott and Andrew Stirling from Adam Purves Mitsubishi, raising funds for my Foundation and Muscular Dystrophy UK.

Our journey started in a G-plate, twenty-eight-year-old Mk1 Shogun, short-wheelbase. The lads at Penryn RFC got us to our pick-up point to collect the old Shogun, and from there we headed to Land's End, on the warmest day of the year, with no air-con. You knew who your best friends were after that first leg.

Then we were all set for the big off. Thankfully we were also provided with a new Mitsubishi L200 – with air-con. Richie and me claimed that, and a tin of Lynx that was kicking about!

After an overnight stop, Gloucester Rugby Club provided a great welcome and breakfast, and we would happily have stayed for brunch and lunch, but we had to get cracking. Eventually, after 933 miles, we made John o'Groats and bed. This was just a brief pit stop, but a big thank you to George Campbell and his son Scott for their hospitality. Because we then took on the North Coast 500 – yes, another five hundred miles – stopping at Ross Sutherland RFC and Caithness RFC to pick up a couple of very generous cheques and to visit Ullapool where incredibly we met ex-Gala prop from the 1960s, Jim Riddell. Richie reckoned that showed how Gala folk were accepted and liked wherever they went. Me, I think he's in hiding.

We saw the beautifully scenic Applecross and stopped at Armadale Farm to see Joyce Campbell, then on to Fort William and the final run for home.

It was around then that the Scottish Rugby Union announced that My Name'5 Doddie Foundation had become one of their official charity partners. There was a wee lump in the throat when I read that, and when I wrote it as well.

A mere 1,561 miles later, we arrived back in the Borders – just in time to make a guest appearance at the Border Union show.

And all of that was a couple days out of my diary.

What was fantastic was hooking up with Richie. Almost exactly thirty years before, we'd been on a Scottish Schools trip to New Zealand and almost didn't have a career to speak of after it. Not the first occasion where I'd proved people wrong.

After that fundraising jaunt, my next assignment was more about saying thank you to a great many people who have assisted me and the family up to this point.

Now, I couldn't possibly publish some of the comments made when I said I would be taking part in the Lauder Common Riding. It wasn't so much that I would like to take part. I was definite about it. Others were equally as vocal in telling me I shouldn't.

To explain, the Common Riding events take place all across the Borders and commemorate an age where the local men and boys would protect their towns and districts from uninvited guests, or protect their stock from cattle thieves – or Reivers as they are called in these parts. Maybe if the south of Scotland's pro rugby team had been called the Borders Cattle Rustlers they'd have attracted more interest.

But the Common Ridings are a really special tradition in the Borders and they have a place in the hearts of everyone who has ever taken part, because for the majority of people it is something they participate in over a lifetime. This year, I was invited (or maybe I invited myself) to participate in the Lauder Common Riding. What could be easier? I've always held myself up as a good horseman and, like riding a bike, you never forget. A lot of this, all of it really, goes back to what my chiropractor, Donald Francis, has been telling me since I started working with him: namely, if you don't use it you lose it.

Being diagnosed with MND, I think a lot of people have gone into a protective state, not wanting to challenge themselves, or wanting to save their energy and strength for other things. I completely get that. But Donald's approach, which I agree with because I've witnessed the benefits of doing my daily routines, is that you can build on what strength you still have.

Now, maybe he didn't mean that in the broadest or most extreme case, namely wrestling with a ton and half of bloodstock, but he didn't tell me not to either. Let's give it a bash then.

What does slip your mind is that a horse, rather than being a bike, is more like a 1000cc superbike, occasionally with a mind of its own. But all I thought I'd have to do was climb aboard and it would all flood back to me. Of course, there were a couple of minor details I had omitted, call it selective amnesia. Firstly, it had been about three years since I'd sat in the saddle, when my niece Alex became Braw Lass – which you might equate to being the Gala Queen in your town or village, except she gets a horse not a carriage – for the Galashiels Common Riding, the Braw Lads Gathering. How much had changed in that time from my perspective? Virtually nothing; well, apart from some of the effects of MND.

Secondly, the time I had ridden before that was probably fifteen, maybe twenty years ago. Think bike. It'll be fine. And it indeed it was fine, having a gentle walk, and a wee trot on a lovely horse owned by John Macfarlane.

That in itself was tremendous. It brought back a lot of memories, of competing in equestrian events, and just sitting that high astride a horse was great. But some of the paths we took, and some of the countryside we rode over, I'd never seen before, even after fifteen years back in these parts. There are bits of the countryside you never see from the road or can't access even in a 4x4, so you don't go near. But, on horseback, you can access the difficult terrain (and even someone's oat field, I do apologise), because of the freedom you have. And that was all very special.

You also have a bit of solitude, quietness from everything else that was going on. The mobile phone was on mute, and you are able to chill and gather your thoughts.

This year, it was fifty years since my auntie Christine, my dad's sister, had been the Lauder Common Riding's Cornet's Lass, and her family have been very supportive of me, so given that anniversary and her help, I decided to reciprocate. Easier said than done – and reciprocate isn't easy to say.

It was a fantastic day, me all dressed up for the part, with a great turnout and a brilliant response from everyone to seeing me there and taking part. The day mostly went without a hitch.

The one difficulty I faced was mounting and dismounting. I needed assistance, but it had to be that I could do it myself. I suppose a crane might have come in handy, but we didn't have one. What we did have, however, was a big box, although I did look like someone had just thrown a big sack of tatties on the back of a horse. Quite undignified, but there were people who could sort me out.

Halfway round, they have the Watering Stane, which, as it sounds, is where riders and their mounts get watered – although I didn't sample much in the way of water. I couldn't spend all afternoon in the saddle, so I had to get off – which meant that the night before, Lee Alexander was sent out into the countryside to secrete a small pair of stepladders behind a wall, so that I could use them to mount up again.

What was nice to see was how many fit and healthy participants also needed them after their pit stop. With that, we headed for home and our ride was going without incident until the final gallop, which was downhill and when it is quite easy for the horse to get away from you slightly.

However, all you need to do is apply the brakes, like a bike. Just pull back on the reins – except that was easier said than done. Three and a half hours in the saddle was a wee bit tiring, and because of that I didn't quite have the strength to pull back, which meant leaning back in the saddle, which causes you to slip forward, which in turn made my head bounce back and forward and I couldn't get my arm up to stop the helmet coming over my eyes.

I'll admit, I was a wee bit disorientated, and I also thought one foot had come out of the stirrup, so there were a few wee palpitations going on, especially when I started overtaking people – or rather, the horse did.

While my mount was galloping along thinking this is good fun, I was thinking maybe this hadn't been such a great plan. As other riders asked if everything was okay as I charged past, I was reassuring other participants, shouting, 'No, I'm fine.' I don't think I was convincing anyone, especially those concerned about my wellbeing.

All this time I was telling myself that, whatever happened, I couldn't fall off, because of the potential consequences. Namely, one, it could and probably would hurt, and two, having to answer the questions about what I was doing on a horse in the first place.

I think the last time I'd had so many things running through my head at that speed, while everything appeared to be taking a while to stop, was when I had that car crash I've mentioned. Scary, I'll admit.

Happily, we landed safely, although I think the horse had had enough as well and wanted a drink, rather like its pilot. No damage, no real dramas (which you would always say anyway), all back in one piece (perhaps with a few bits hingin' off) and a grand day was had by all. Wonderful to support and be supported. Until next time, when I'll wear gloves – I'd forgotten how sweaty the reins get – and I might carry a land anchor as well, just as a precaution.

A week later, and not feeling entirely match fit (my neck and shoulders were still a bit achy after my ride), I swapped four legs for two wheels and took part in Doddie'5 Ride, a cycle run for all, brilliantly organised by Peter Winterbottom, the brains behind the Ride with the Legends events.

Having launched the day at the Greenyards earlier in the summer, along with Wints and with the help of the lovely and very talented Louise Haston, a multiple Commonwealth and Masters champion, we waited as the entries rolled in, eventually registering over 650 competitors of all shapes and sizes. That description especially applied to my big pal Stuart Grimes, who arrived with a tandem. This was so typical of him, having someone else share the workload.

He was exactly the same when I was playing beside him for Scotland and Newcastle. To be fair, he was accompanied by his young daughter, and then he went out and did another couple of miles two or three times so various nieces and nephews could also be presented with a medal.

Sadly, a front-wheel puncture and subsequent wheel collapse meant his last run turned into a sponsored walk.

Unfortunately, the summer sun had given way to torrential rain, but no one appeared too bothered by that. There were people from the north of Scotland, Portsmouth, even Ireland, joining in with a host of international stars who had turned out on the day: Craig Chalmers (who is quite a serious rider on Legends events), Roger Uttley, Dean Richards, Rodger Arneil, Iwan Tukalo, Scott Hastings, Keith Robertson, Gordon Hunter, Alan Tomes, Gary Armstrong, Scott Wight and Rob Wainwright, who, having completed the first half of the course himself, then partnered me over the second leg, just to make sure I got home safely.

If I have missed anyone from that off-the-top-of-my-head list, then I do apologise, but my memory lapse is almost entirely down to seeing Carl Hogg in Lycra, something he normally only keeps for 'Jill with a J'.

My role on the day was to be more ceremonial than anything, meeting and greeting, lending support, and flagging away the competitors on both runs: the eleven-mile family ride, favoured by the slightly less adventurous and mad-keen youngsters alike, and the tougher sixty-miler, which took in a huge part of the Borders countryside.

While being encouraged to do the lesser (only in terms of mileage) of the two runs, I wasn't having any of that.

So many had turned out, I thought it only right that after flagging everyone off, I was dropped off somewhere out on the course, around the halfway point, so as many fellow cyclists and members of the public who had turned out to spectate could see me participating and allow me to say thanks to them.

What some may not know – and this might blow my cover now – was that I had acquired a rather special battery powered bike. Now before you think that was cheating, I pedalled the route and only used the battery for the uphill sections, especially the last climb into Melrose, which I rocketed up like Geraint Thomas. Those who didn't know my bike was independently powered must have been impressed.

In saying that, the boys from Hawick Cycle Club impressed everyone, blasting around the course in two hours forty-seven minutes. That was for sixty miles, not eleven.

It was a fantastic day, and again thanks to Peter and his team for putting in all the hard graft.

After a busy week, I was able to take a deep breath and relax, back in the clubrooms at the Greenyards with a couple of the boys, having a damn good laugh and wondering how or if we were going to get home. The best kind of day, and the smile on my face said it all, or nearly said it all.

Once again, a great many people had come out to support me. It was only proper that I put a bit of an effort in myself.

However, that evening, I wanted to give a wee pump of the fist, punch the air, and have a celebratory shout to myself. Because whether I should have ridden a horse, or a bike, was neither here nor there now. It was done, I'd done it, and like a few other things in the last eighteen months,

I had bucked convention, proved the experts wrong, and proved to myself and others that there might be another way to kick back against this MND, taking it on, head on, and giving two fingers to this dreadful condition.

I'd never shirked a challenge or confrontation on the rugby pitch and I've never had any intention of doing that now. So, here's to the other challenges I might set myself, or have set for me. I'm up for the fight because I still have things – short and long term – that I'd like to be here for.

I have a few TV engagements coming off with Premier Sport covering the PRO14 this season, and with BT Sport for matches in the Gallagher Premiership. Those were offers I hadn't expected, and it really gave me some fantastic pieces of news to come home from holiday to. The Doddie Weir Cup in November 2018, Wales versus Scotland, is another cast-iron date in my diary. How good is that going to be, presenting a trophy with my name on it when the norm is for you to be commemorated in that way when you have long gone. I hope it's a big cup. Not for show, but so that it takes a bit of filling.

These things spur you on because others, to my mind, have been less fortunate. I was at the funeral of Finlay Calder's brother, Gavin, who died on the golf course just over a year ago. A few times that day, as people said their farewells, I heard it mentioned about it being a great way to go, doing something he enjoyed. And I get that. But were there things that Gavin would have wanted to see or hear, or do or fulfil before he left this earth? I'd imagine there might have been, and I think that would be the same for most people.

Me, I'm different. I know I might be going sooner than expected, so there are things I want to do, places I want to go, and things I want to see, some of those being quite mundane under normal circumstances, but then these aren't normal times. It is my intention to get to do them.

I'm lucky that I was here to see Hamish pass his driving test. I never thought that would happen. Not him taking to the roads – and what a great chauffeur he's become for me and his mum – but me being around to witness him achieving one of his goals in life. It was much the same when he left school.

Similarly, I was so delighted seeing Angus pass his tractor driving test, and Ben playing age-group district rugby. Wee things, in the grand scheme of things, but each of them so very special, just because I got to see it.

I don't so much have a bucket list. No, you can only get so much in a bucket. I've gone instead for a tank – a silage tank!

It has meant a rather hectic schedule on occasions. For instance, I was hoping to take maybe June and July off. But when you are invited to Royal Ascot or to visit the Scottish Open golf tournament to see so many of the players sporting tartan trews in the My Name'5 Doddie Foundation tartan, or get an invite to join Her Majesty, the Queen, at her garden party at Holyrood Palace, you don't say no.

Richard Scott had me down at the British Grand Prix at Silverstone, where I got to meet so many lovely people – and we're not just talking about my pals Lee McKenzie and Natalie Pinkham here. Another great experience.

I'm thankful that I've been able to tick things off that

weren't even on my list (or in my tank) when I was given the devastating news about MND. I'm so lucky to have been given those opportunities, although with one or two, Kathy has told me, 'Aye, you're going,' entirely because she quite fancies it as well. And who can blame her.

I'd love to, in about ten years' time, after all the speaking, travelling, partying, eating, drinking, meeting the most fantastic people, inspirational individuals and generous human beings, turn around and say it's all been a huge hoax, I just couldn't be bothered working again and just wanted to have a good time.

Actually, if I'm still here in ten years' time I might just do it for the sheer hell of it.

Sadly, this is no hoax. This is very real.

This is where I've found my friends, associates, ex-teammates and players, and acquaintances since I've started having my issues, invaluable, none more so than my business partner at Hutchinson's, Pete Stedman, my right-hand man (and left-hand more often than not) Lee Alexander, and the rest of the team. Much of my workload over the last twenty months has dropped on their desk, allowing my gallivanting – I mean hard work on behalf of the Foundation – to continue, although they'd probably say I didn't do that much to begin with.

During that time, I really have begun to realise just how many people I know and have met, or have the mobile number for, or know someone else who can contact them.

I've never been great remembering names. I've had so many conversations over thirty years, where I must have appeared as though I was listening intently to what people were saying, when all I was doing was waiting on them to give me a clue as to who they were, what their name was or where we'd met. A terrible confession, I know, and I apologise to those people I've been unable to identify or call by their name.

However, ironically, since being diagnosed with MND, I've become a lot better at identifying folk and faces and putting names to them. It's been a wee exercise I've been playing with myself, I don't know, perhaps to see if the hard-drive upstairs still has the capacity to save and store things, and then regurgitate them.

It all seems to be fine, and I've started listening very carefully to what people are saying to me more recently as well, especially those in the medical profession. Hearing that you may only have so long to live does focus the mind, not that I would recommend seeking out that kind of news.

I have, I think, always treated everyone the same, the way I'd want them to treat me. I've never gone out my way to impress, or talk differently to a sir or a lord, to a lawyer or an accountant, any differently than I have a farmer at market, or someone serving me in a shop, or pointing me in the right direction at the train station. For one thing, I'd soon be found out if I tried, but also, at some point I have needed, or may need, their help or company. That could be especially true if you are lying in a hospital bed.

Sport, and in my case rugby, has been great for making you aware of just how reliant you are on others. I believe that's why people have been friendly towards me, which I'm grateful for, even more so today, but also why so many across the country, and indeed the world, have been so forthcoming with offers of help and assistance.

When you see the likes of Russell Kelsey pedalling from Twickenham to Edinburgh in just forty-four hours before the Calcutta Cup game, or Gordon Bulloch running up a mountain umpteen times to equal the height of Everest, or have guys investing in a racehorse called Behindthelines and donating the winnings to the Foundation, you can't help thinking that you are a very fortunate human being to have friends and associates like that.

And I couldn't list those who have hosted quizzes, dressed up at school and work, walked, run and cycled mega miles, or baked cakes. Some of them, as my expanding waistline would suggest, have been very tasty indeed. Again, thank you a million times, or make that two million.

Which is why, after just a year, by September 2018, the My Name'5 Doddie Foundation has raised and distributed over £1 million of funding.

Amazing, and the biggest thank you possible to all the fantastic people out there who have donated and helped. But we are not finished.

I am continuing, with the help of real experts in the field, to try and find a cure, or something that halts the onset and progression of MND in its tracks. Unfortunately, much of what I've found until now is frustration, that there is nothing out there, in terms of drugs and, on occasions, basic guidance and assistance.

If I can help, push or challenge those inadequacies faced by all victims of Motor Neurone Disease, then it will be job done.

My diagnosis with MND, and everything that surrounds it, has become a not-insignificant part of my life. It is, however, only a small episode in my forty-eight years to date. How would I describe things currently? How about highs, lows and laughter? Pretty much as my life has always been, perhaps best typified by a story from a while ago.

After a day at Murrayfield and a night with old pals and enemies in Edinburgh, I left it a bit too close for comfort when catching the last train to Tweedbank. Charging down the stairs at Waverley, I had about a minute to run three hundred yards, which in a tartan suit, brogues and with a suit carrier over my shoulder, wasn't easy, but amazingly I made it. A high.

At Tweedbank, I said farewell to the assorted folks who had been up at the England game, and thanked the driver, explaining that I'd only just made the train with a performance that Usain Bolt would have been proud of.

'Ach, you were fine. Seeing it's the last train, I always wait a few minutes for stragglers before I leave,' he explained.

From a high to a low.

But that was quickly followed by the laughter. Who was I kidding, covering that distance in sixty seconds? No one, especially the driver – but he didn't have to spoil it!

Life, with or without MND, summed up in one act. Highs, lows and laughter.

Whatever happens in the future, I've had the best wake anyone could ever have had. It's been an amazing journey up to this point, still partying, still drinking, still lasting the night out better than most.

And long may it continue.

Acknowledgements

DODDIE WEIR

O F EVERYTHING IN THIS BOOK, this is perhaps the most difficult part, given I have limited space, probably deliberately, otherwise we might run into a second volume just on mentions alone.

There are quite literally thousands of people I must thank on behalf of myself, my family, the Trust and the My Name'5 Doddie Foundation. Most of them I don't even know, or have just met or played against once. They are people who have supported all the activities set up to raise funds so that the Foundation might help others to battle Motor Neurone Disease. Similarly, there are a number of individuals who have chosen to remain behind the scenes, who have been generous in their support of me and the Foundation, and to them I say, I owe you a debt of gratitude and a drink.

To all of my rugby colleagues – across the international and club teams we've played for, or played against, or been coached and managed by, and in the media as well – the 'rugby family' has shown in their support that we have a sport like no other. This applies equally to the Scottish Rugby Union, where Dominic McKay and Graham Law have assisted greatly.

Special thanks as well to Jim Telfer and his kind words in the Foreword. Had he said these things thirty years ago I could have been inspired to work harder and may even have tried to enjoy training.

My business partner Pete Stedman has taken on so much of late, as has everyone else at Hutchinson Environmental Solutions. Pete, who I have worked with for the last fifteen years, has been amazingly supportive from day one, and has kept the business going – probably for the last fifteen years! 'Thank you' will never be enough and I wish Pete, Alison and Jack, and all the Hutchinson staff and clients every success in the future.

I could replicate those sentiments for the trustees for the Trust and Foundation – Scott Hastings, Gary Armstrong, Finlay Calder, John Jeffrey, Jill Douglas and Stewart Weir, and for all the work they have put in – but I won't, as I am fed up with being told 'away and don't be daft' every time I've tried to say it in the past. What they have done, however, with help from the likes of Kenny Logan, Jim Robertson, Addleshaw Goddard, Hampden & Co and The Digital Age, has been indispensable and immense.

Special thanks to Stewart Weir for helping me finally get this book written. He's been there or thereabouts for the last twenty years and knows me all too well, but without his constant cajoling and his way with words this book would not have happened any time soon.

To Mum and Dad, Nanny and Jock, Kirsty and Douglas, Thomas and Anne, Christopher and Laura, Kathy's family, George and Violet, Jane, Sarah and Graeme, Gina and Bruce, and all our nieces and nephews, you have been so fantastic.

Last, and certainly never least, my wife Kathy and wonderful boys Hamish, Angus and Ben. Maybe not the way we planned it, but we are where we are and we've had a good time getting here. Love and thank you x

STEWART WEIR

'WHY DON'T WE DO A BOOK?'
It seemed a good idea. Doddie was easily one of the most recognisable rugby personalities in Scotland, indeed across the British Isles. A winner with Newcastle, and a favourite with Lions fans as a star of the *Living With Lions* video. He had a great story to tell.

Dod had kept something of a diary, not entirely accurate, but it had all the key pointers, I had most of the notes from ghosting his columns over the years, and, anyway, his mum, Nanny, had an Aladdin's cave of cuttings from when he first played at school. I wanted to write more and Doddie aimed to rest up during the summer to charge the batteries. What was stopping us?

This was May 2000.

Wind forward almost exactly eighteen years and, as we

head for a speaking engagement in Coventry, I finally press the record button and begin chatting to Dodgy, amid much hilarity that we were finally doing this.

'What kept you?' Doddie laughs, to which I reply, 'Aye, I could ask the same thing.'

An offer from Ali and Campbell at Black & White Publishing focused our thinking, although not as much as a change in circumstance. So, here it is, finally, arguably a better yarn for the delay, but with a twist none of us saw coming.

This summer has been spent trying to capture Doddie's life, career and emotions. In reality it was spent trying to capture him. Nailing jelly to a wall would have been easier. But perseverance, unfathomable hours, and various references to a contract paid off, and now we have a book.

To that end, my love, thanks and a promise that I will make it up to you goes to Nicola, Gillian, Louise, Callum and Zara, for their support, encouragement and simply leaving me to get on with it.

It goes without saying that it was an honour being asked to work on this book by my big pal, who I love to bits, and admire even more. And I imagine, in that last sentence, I have the privilege of communicating those feelings on behalf of every rugby fan, follower and player the world over.

Player Profile
DODDIE WEIR

Position
Lock

Height
6 foot 6 inches

Melrose
Championship (winner) 1989/90, 1991/92,
1992/93, 1993/94, 1995/96

Newcastle Falcons
Championship (winner) 1997/98
Cup (winner) 2000/2001

Scotland
1990–2000, winning a total of 61 caps (four tries)
Five Nations Championship (winner) 1999

British & Irish Lions
South Africa 1997 (three matches, one try)

Barbarians
1992–2002 (six matches, one try)

The
MY NAME'5 DODDIE
Foundation

DODDIE SHARED HIS MND diagnosis with the world in June 2017. From the outset he was determined to help others affected by this devastating disease, driven by his frustration at the lack of progress in treatment, and the absence of options for those given this awful prognosis.

This led Doddie and key supporters to establish the My Name'5 Doddie Foundation, launched at Murrayfield ahead of the Scotland versus New Zealand match in November 2017.

The My Name'5 Doddie Foundation has set basic targets: to raise awareness around MND, help find a cure and support those affected by the disease.

Simply put, this is a race against time for all sufferers. The disease kills a third of people within a year and more than half within two and a half years of diagnosis.

The response to Doddie's appeal has been incredible, generating huge support, both financially and from many fellow MND sufferers and their families, often simply looking to make contact and share their experiences and take courage from Doddie's approach, his openness and positivity.

On the one-year anniversary of the launch of the My Name'5 Doddie Foundation, we have committed £1 million to research projects to find a cure for Motor Neurone Disease and to support those affected by it, and have commissioned an independent report to help steer our strategy going forward, to continue to challenge the medical research community.

We have established relationships with MND Association and MND Scotland to help administer grants to those who need our support. In addition, we consider one-off assistance payments to help individuals in desperate need of practical support.

My Name'5 Doddie Foundation are hugely excited to be moving into our second year and to see how we can continue to raise awareness of MND and work towards helping find a cure.

For more information, see www.myname5doddie.co.uk.

The Trustees
September 2018